D0994916

Active
in Orange County

A Guide to
Physical Activity
and Exercise
in Nature

Nanda Fischer • Jutta Gamboa

Publishing

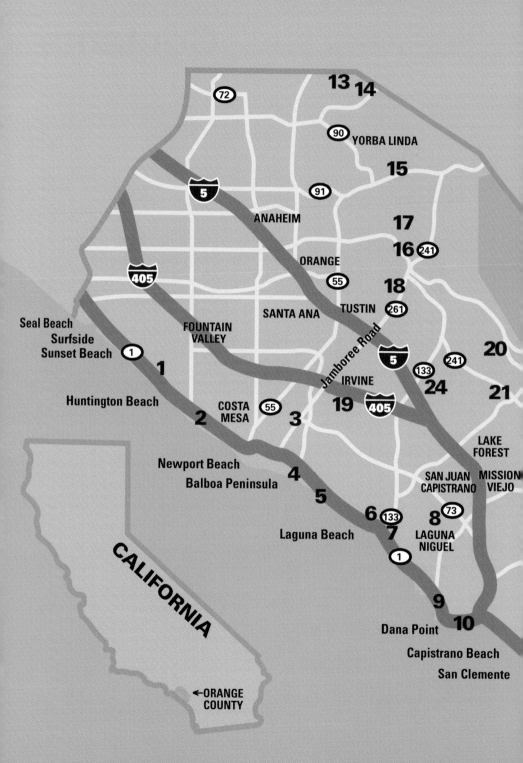

ORANGE COUNTY
Regional and State Parks and Beaches

1) Bolsa Chica State Beach/Nature Preserve
2) Huntington State Beach
3) Upper Newport Bay Ecological Reserve
4) Corona Del Mar State Beach
5) Crystal Cove State Park
6) Laguna Coast Wilderness Park
7) Aliso and Wood Canyons Regional Park
8) Laguna Niguel Regional Park
9) Salt Creek County Beach and Bluff Park
10) Doheny State Beach
11) Calafia State Beach Park
12) San Clemente State Beach
13) Carbon Canyon Regional Park
14) Chino Hills State Park
15) Yorba Regional Park
16) Irvine Regional Park
17) Santiago Oaks Regional Park
18) Peters Canyon Regional Park
19) William Mason Regional Park
20) Limestone Canyon and Whiting
    Ranch Wilderness Park
21) O'Neill Regional Park
22) Thomas O'Riley Wilderness Park
23) Caspers Park
24) Orange County Great Park

SANTA ANA MOUNTAINS

TRABUCO
CANYON

CLEVELAND
NF

RANCHO
SANTA
MARGERITA

23

22

74

11

12

1. Introduction

Intention of the Authors

Nanda Fischer   *Jutta Gamboa*

A couple of years ago a friend came up with a great idea: "What if we get an outdoor exercise group going? We meet once or twice a week and do different activities each time."

We had been complaining about our limited exercise possibilities, since we did not like going to the gym very much, but were keen to exercise. We shared a love for the outdoors. Here, in beautiful Southern California we hardly ever have to deal with the weather. What could be healthier and more fun than exploring the diverse nature and working up a sweat at the same time?

Enthusiastically, we started our outdoor program in various attractive areas of Orange County. We would be active between one to two and a half hours and often, for an added bonus, finish with a healthy snack or lunch.

When our spouses and friends saw us enjoy our activities so immensely, they joined our group. Everybody had new ideas and suggestions for areas to go to and be active. For many activities we could take our children along.

Over the years we have discovered abundant opportunities in Orange County for exercising in open space. Thus the idea was born to make our experiences accessible to other active people.

This guide is meant to suggest scenic areas for outdoor activities for residents of Orange County, who have not had the chance to discover them yet, for the newcomer to Orange County, and of course, for visitors.

We address people seeking moderate to advanced exercise, active families and athletic adventurers.

We pride ourselves in suggesting a great variety of physical activities. On the one hand we believe each activity supplies a unique experience, and on the other hand we are aware that different activities give the body a more complete training than one kind of activity can provide. We exclude most commercial offers.

We concentrate on informal self guided activities in open space in and on the water and on trails. Nevertheless, we also include opportunities on public grounds for more formal outdoor sports activities like tennis, volleyball, skateboarding, golf, and even archery.

We inform you, where community facilities are offered, where you can use them without charge, or where you have to pay a fee.

We hope you will have as much fun exercising in the outdoors, as we always do, while at the same time enjoying our beautiful land.

Finally, let us mention that Nanda Fischer as a cancer surviver attributes her wellness to the "positive" stress she has experienced while regularly exercising in the outdoors.

Last but not least we want to express our thanks to family members and friends who contributed with advice and suggestions to the book.

Special thanks to Conrad Whitaker, who brushed up our English where it was necessary.

Nanda Fischer   Jutta Gamboa

How to Use This Guide

The book is divided into two parts. In part one we cover activities in coastal areas, in part two we deal with activities in inland areas of Orange County. Each part reads from north to south. Subdivisions are: activities on and in the water (mostly on the coast), trail activities (mostly in wilderness parks and nature preserves), and more formal sports activities (mostly in city parks or recreational facilities provided by the communities or non profit organizations).

We try to be comprehensive as to the "Beach Cities".

Inland we select just the "jewels" of the many opportunities in Orange County.

With city parks and other outdoor recreational facilities we are even more selective.

For each location of any given activity we offer a description of its natural features as well as additional information that contributes to the profile of a beach, a trail or a park.

Also, we indicate what time of the year or of the day is best for an activity at a given location, and, where applicable, the skill level it requires.

We explain how to get there, where to park, inform you about fees, or how to avoid them, and most often suggest a place for a snack, a lunch or a coffee afterwards.

For your convenience we also include maps for easier access to activity sites. Detailed maps of all the trails of a park are handed out at park headquarters. You will also find most trail maps of Orange County's parks in the internet: www.ocparks.com

Special Features and Other Attractions

We highlight the special features a given area or park offers, from stunning views to great campgrounds, to good places to observe wildlife and flora.

We also note some of the most worthwhile cultural attractions in the area, in case you want to combine your physical activity with visiting one or the other interesting landmark or event.

Fees, Operating Times, Phone Numbers, and Websites

Policies change, and so do prices and phone numbers. Therefore, we have mostly avoided quoting exact fees, operating times or phone numbers. As a rule, parks are open from dawn to dusk.

If you plan to visit a public beach or park for the first time, we recommend checking their website. We included the most important web addresses.

Rating

Even though rating is very subjective, we dare anyhow and rate beaches, trails, or parks on a one to five scale (five being the highest) according to our overall impression, with special consideration of the scenic beauty of the area and the opportunity for a variety of activities on all levels.

●●●●● Superb – an extraordinary area for the chosen activities.

●●●●◖ Very good – a far above average area.

●●●● Good - a very nice area.

●●●◖ Average – a nice area.

●●● Fair – and in some way below standard. area, but nevertheless worthwhile going.

●●◖ An area below standard, not recommended.

Feedback

We have visited every site several times and participated in all the activities suggested. We don't expect that you share all of our opinions. Therefore, we would welcome a feedback from you, a comment or a new suggestion.

Email: fandb.publisher@googlemail.com
Website: activeinoc-fandb.com

2. Orange County

Newport Beach harbor ....

... and paddlers in the harbor in front of Balboa Pavilion almost one hundred years ago

The gardens of Mission San Juan Capistrano at present

Orange County Cultural History

Orange County formally came into existence in 1889, when the three communities Anaheim, Santa Ana and Orange by demand of their leaders separated from LA County. However, the 786 square mile area has a long history of inhabitation.

Native Americans dwelled on the coast and in the lower canyons probably since at least 4000 BCE.

In founding Mission San Juan Capistrano in 1776, one of the 21 Franciscan missions established in California, the Spanish began the colonization of Orange County.

Father Junipero Serra, had come with Gasper de Portola in his undertaking to claim California for Spain. Under his leadership the Native Americans of Orange County converted to Christianity, partly so, since only converted Native Americans could own land. They were also used as cheap labor for the mission.

When Mexico gained its independence from Spain in 1821, only Mexicans could become landowners. And when in 1833 the missions were secularized by the Mexicans, land holdings of the mission were parceled out in ranches and given as grants to former war heroes and aristocrats.

On Sept.1 1850, California became the thirty first state of the Union. Again, land in Orange County changed hands. When the occupants could not show the US required documents of ownership, the state took those parcels of land and then sold them cheaply to farmers and ranchers, mostly from the east.

Later, a severe drought caused many farmers to go bankrupt. Thus, finally, very few Native Americans and simple farmers were left owning land. Instead, big parcels of Orange County went to a few families, who invested in Real Estate. James Irvine, for instance, became sole owner of about a fifth of Orange County (120 000 acres) and made Irvine Ranch a flowering enterprise. Nowadays the Irvine Company is one of the largest enterprises in the county.

Early successful settlements like Anaheim (1857), former Campo Alemano founded by German immigrants and Santa Ana (1869), presently county seat, became centers of cattle farms and agriculture.

Citrus fruits were a favorite, due to the mild climate: In 1889 there were 150 000 orange trees in the area, thus the name Orange County.

With a population of close to 400 000 each, they are still the two largest cities in Orange County. Anaheim became also a tourist center, when Disneyland was established in 1955. Santa Ana is well known for its Bowers Museum.

Spawned by oil discoveries in the Huntington Beach area industrialization progressed in the twentieth century. Also Aerospace Industry and Semiconductor Technology found its place in Orange County.

Entertainment business from Hollywood ventured out to adjacent Orange County, filming on locations in Huntington Beach, Newport Beach, and Laguna Beach. Disneyland set stage for other theme parks like Knott's Berry Farm in Buena Park.

Costa Mesa stands out with its Performing Arts Center close to the border of Newport Beach. Irvine with its ambitious UCI campus, that employs several recent Nobel Prize laureates, and the Mission in San Juan Capistrano, further add cultural value and diversity to the area.

Bells and ruins, Mission San Juan Capistrano

Balboa Pavilion, Newport Beach

Entertainment business at the beach

Barkley Theater at UC Irvine

Advertisement for Orange County's Valencia oranges

Orange County as Part of Southern California

Even though Orange County is the smallest of the coastal counties of Southern California, the almost fifty mile shoreline is surely outstanding. Whether you are out for wide sandy beaches, rocky shores, tide pools, underwater riffs, coves, or towering bluffs, that give you seemingly endless views of the Pacific Ocean, Orange County has it all.

Since North Orange County is part of the Los Angeles Basin, it is mostly flat with wide sandy beaches.

Central and most of South Orange County is hilly to mountainous, and on the coast sandy coves are hidden below steep and mostly rocky cliffs.

Inland, the rugged Santa Ana Mountains rise over 5000 feet, and invite you to physical activities that are rewarded with sweeping views.

Orange County's coastal climate is also outstanding: lots of sunshine, mild in winter with occasional rain, warm, but hardly ever hot in summer.

The average high coastal temperature in January is 63.5 degrees Fahrenheit, the average high temperature in August is 73.2 degrees.

The further you get inland, the warmer it gets in the summer. A few miles can make a big difference: average high temperatures inland go up to well over 80 degrees in August. In winter inland areas stay on the cooler and sometimes even on the frostier side.

Water temperatures in Orange County fluctuate between 58 degrees in January and 70 degrees in August.

The Coastline and the Beach Cities of Orange County

To the outdoor person the forty plus miles of Orange County's coastline from Seal Beach in the north to San Clemente in the south are of special interest.

Seal Beach, Surfside and Sunset Beach are the three northernmost beach communities in Orange County, where the nice sandy beaches are mostly populated by locals.

Seal Beach is noteworthy also for its wildlife sanctuary. Sunset Beach attracts kite surfers.

The first outstanding Beach City in northern Orange County is adjacent Huntington Beach or "Surf City USA", which hosts the US Open of surfing. Its eight miles of uninterrupted wide beaches are evenly attractive to surfers and swimmers of all ages and abilities. Its impressive pier stretches more than 1800 feet out into the Pacific Ocean.

Along the boardwalk that runs parallel to the shoreline, trail activities are very popular.

Huntington Central Park, which covers more than 350 acres, offers numerous activities from horseback riding to frisbee golf.

For the outdoor enthusiast Huntington Beach is therefore one of the top spots to be active all year in Orange County.

From the many beach cities that boom since the mid 20th century, Laguna Beach and Newport Beach, which border Crystal Cove State Park to the north and south respectively, stand out.

Newport Beach started to gain its reputation at the end of the 19th century, when summer guests put up their tents on sandy Balboa Peninsula and when McFadden had his railroad line come to the wharf on Balboa Peninsula.

In the mid thirties of the last century, after the Santa Ana River was diverted the city's yacht harbor, a true marvel was finished. It is one of the leading yacht harbors of today. And whether you tour it by boat or cross it with the old fashioned ferry, which connects Balboa Peninsula to Balboa Island, the many a yachts,

Kite surfing at Sunset Beach

Don't be mislead by the name Orange County and look for oranges other than in supermarkets. Almost all of the orange groves are gone. Instead, about three million people are living nowadays in over forty cities.

However, there are still enough nature pockets left to get away from it all. Surprisingly, the disadvantages of Orange County are at the same time its advantages. Everything from Disneyland to the opera, to county and state parks protecting the open space, is very close.

Huntington Beach Pier

the sparkling waters and the seabirds all over the area, make it a truly picturesque scene.

Furthermore, sandy beaches, impressive bluffs, and the famous Back Bay which hosts thousands of migrating birds in winter add to the attraction of Newport Beach.

The many very well kept city parks offer abundant opportunities for more formal sports activities.

Well known Fashion Island Shopping Center, the upscale housing, the vicinity to Los Angeles, also contribute to making Newport Beach with a population of roughly 80 000 one of the most sought after places in California.

Little Corona Beach in Newport Beach

Crystal Cove State Park is stretching from the southern border of Newport Beach to Laguna Beach. It covers over three miles of natural seashore and 2.400 acres of undeveloped woodland of canyons and foothills. Besides having fun on the beach and in the water, you can hike, ride horses, run or bike for hours and often not meet a single other person. It is a piece of paradise left in the otherwise busy neighborhood.

Laguna Beach, southern neighbor to Newport Beach, with its many art galleries is a permanent host of the Festival of the Arts and other significant arts events.

Treasure Point, Crystal Cove Beach

Steep bluffs and numerous sandy beaches hiding below in spectacular coves make this part of Orange County one of the most scenic in California. The many motels and seaside resorts tell of the summer and winter guests, who seek out Laguna Beach as their favorite vacation spot.

Laguna Coast Wilderness Park is located between Crystal Cove State Park in the north Aliso and Wood Canyons Wilderness Park in the southeast; thus making the Laguna Beach area also a hiking, mountain biking, and equestrian paradise.

Dana Point to the south of Laguna Beach is a rather new urban development, The men made yacht harbor with its over 2500 boat slips, drove away the surfers, who considered the beach one of their favorites.

Heisler Park, Laguna Beach

San Clemente in South Orange County

The harbor of Dana Point, view from Heritage Park

Doheny State Beach in the south of the city is nowadays known for its calmer, rather warm waters.

Capistrano Beach, the next city to the southeast of Dana Point, is a small beach community. Due to the spectacular neighboring beach cities and busy PCH running right along the coast it is mostly frequented by locals.

Don't miss San Clemente at the southern end of Orange County, nestled in hills above the cliffs. It managed to preserve its Spanish style charm. It is a favorite for surfers. Among the many sandy beaches in the city, San Clemente State Beach is one of Orange County's preferred sites.

The "Sinks", Limestone-Whiting Ranch Park

Inland Areas

The many regional parks of Orange County and the wilderness areas of the Santa Ana Mountains are our choice for activities in inland areas.

In this guide we are focusing on trail activities in the wilderness areas, but we also suggest some formal sports activities at selected sites.We proceed from North to South Orange County.

In North Orange County we suggest trail activities in the greater area of Yorba Linda, a city, which is known for its park like setting and its very scenic public golf course.

Spring on a trail in the foothills

North of the city you will find Carbon Canyon Regional Park, which connects to Chino Hills Park with many attractive trails. Carbon Canyon Park is noteworthy, because it hosts Southern California's only redwood grove.

Yorba Regional Park, to the south and adjacent to the Santa Ana River, not only features abundant opportunities for the sports enthusiast, but also connects to the Pacific Ocean via the Santa Ana River Bike Trail.

Central Orange County offers great opportunities for the outdoor activist. Three important Central Orange County parks are located within the boundaries of the city of Orange. Its town center is worth visiting.

Santa Ana Mountains

Hiking in Santa Ana Mountains

Rock in Ronald W. Caspers Wilderness Park

Santiago Oaks Regional Park connects to the Anaheim Hills trail system in the Santa Ana Mountains.

Irvine Regional Park is California's first county park and offers abundant trails to hikers, bikers and horseback riders.

Peters Canyon Regional Park, a nice area for hiking and mountain biking is the third park in this area. It is also the starting point for the "From Mountains to Sea" bike trail.

East of these parks in the Santa Ana Mountains we suggest trail activities in Modjeska Canyon, Black Star Canyon and Silverado Canyon, where a challenging hike goes up to Bedford Peak (3800 feet), Buena Vista Trail and Holy Jim Trail.

Irvine, adjacent to Newport Beach and host to the University of California (UCI) offers neither an ocean nor mountains, but is a great place for active people. It features not only William R. Mason Regional Park but also numerous community parks offering opportunities for almost any sport you can think of. Furthermore, there are many scenic trails going through the city and beyond its boundaries.

The Southern Foothills of the Santa Ana Mountains offer many trails for hikers and mountain bikers. Limestone Canyon and Whiting Ranch Wilderness Park offer Little Grand Canyon and the great scenery of Red Rock Canyon.

O'Neill Regional Park is favored by equestrians as well as further inland located Thomas F. Riley Wilderness Park .

Several trails from this area lead into the wilderness and to Santiago Peak (5.687 feet).

In South Orange County within the inland area of San Juan Capistrano we explore expansive Ronald W. Caspers Wilderness Park with (equestrian) camp grounds and a great variety of trails for hikers, horseback riders and mountain bikers alike.

We strongly recommend a visit to Mission San Juan Capistrano.

Active in Orange County

- Archery • Baseball • Basketball • Biking • Body Surfing • Boogie Boarding
- Canoeing • Frisbee Golf • Equestrian • Handball • Hiking • Inline Skating
- Jogging • Kayaking • Kite Surfing • Lawn Bowling • Mountain Biking
- Rowing • Sailing • Scuba Diving • Skateboarding • Skimboarding • Snorkeling
- Soccer • Softball • Surfing • Swimming • Tennis • Track • Volleyball
- Walking • Wind Surfing • Yoga

Orientation

Due to its climate and its topography Orange County is the place for active people.

With the exception of winter sports any outdoor physical activity can be performed here.

In this guide we cover over thirty different activities from archery to yoga. However, we do not attempt to be comprehensive.

Since there are so many opportunities for very common activities like baseball or soccer, we will mention sites, but do not go into details.

We prefer self guided to organized activities and we concentrate on free to low cost opportunities. If you are interested in organized activities, look for offerings by the YMCA, the Sierra Club, and other non-profit organizations.

Also, community recreation departments in Orange County offer a variety of physical activities or classes, usually for a nominal fee.

Last but not least, there are numerous commercial enterprises in Orange County that offer tours or teach physical activities, though they are rather pricy.

In general, our two hour and a half time frame excludes time consuming activities. Nevertheless, we will suggest a few all day activities (XXL), as they are very worthwile.

A beautiful community park

A soccer game works anywhere

Venues

Nothing is greater than to exercise in the open country. However, not too much open space is left in Orange County.

The Santa Ana Mountains provide the most extensive wilderness area in the County.

State, county, regional, city and neighborhood parks nowadays mostly preserve natural settings. Some of these parks are almost completely left as wilderness areas. Often trails from these parks lead into surrounding wilderness, thus extending your choice of trips.

In other parks you can explore the wilderness as well as being active in more formal sports like volleyball or tennis.

In the many community and neighborhood parks of Orange County you often have the choice of almost any sport.

Community recreational facilities, sports facilities of schools and colleges, as well those of non profit organizations provide further opportunities to exercise outdoors for a minimal charge or for free.

Health and Safety Hints

Health Awareness
Exercising in general is very healthy. However, under certain conditions it can be unhealthy.

Exercising on the beach

The Orange County Register publishes the times of high and low tides. Local tide booklets are also available for free at many equipment shops near the beaches.

Often it is best to arrange your activities around the low tide hours.

Jellyfish sometimes can be found in summer months. However, in Orange County, they are rather rare. They are interesting to observe, but avoid touching them, since their tentacle bites do burn. Also urchins and stingrays can cause a problem, if you step on them. They are mostly found in surf areas that are rather rocky.

If you observe the following rules, you should be safe.

1. As an outdoor activist you need regular medical checkups, to make sure health conditions permit you to exercise at your usual level.
2. Know your limits. Don't overdo, just because others in your company have different limits. Don't try to match them.
3. More is not always better. This rule applies especially to the older athlete.
4. Exercising different areas of your body rather than specializing too much helps to avoid injuries.
5. Nothing speaks against daily exercising, if you are sports addicted. But if you feel tired over a longer period of time, it mostly is not because you are in bad shape, but because you exercise too often or too intensely.

If you go swimming, consult locals or life guards about hidden rocks, rip tides, or under currents. Also, if you are not an expert swimmer, avoid areas where, or days when the surf is strong.

If you need equipment for your water activity, make sure the equipment is in top shape.

If you are boating, a life vest for every person in the boat is a must. Also, be aware of boat traffic in harbors.

Surfing under piers can be life threatening. Also, surfers can be very territorial. So be careful as a newcomer.

If you go scuba diving, make absolutely sure that your equipment is in top shape, and go with a companion, if possible.

Safety at Water Activities

Most of your water activities in Orange County are in or on the ocean. Therefore, consulting tide tables is a must for many activities, such as scuba diving, snorkeling, kayaking, surfing, and the like.

Even for hiking along the beach you need the tide tables, since some beach hikes can only be done at minus tides, since beaches are impassable at high tide.

Life guards watch over OC beaches

Two friends return from scuba diving

Company is fun and makes the trip safer

In general, in case you are not an expert in any water activity, either go together with an expert, or have an expert instruct you to a degree that you are safe when out on your own, in or on the water.

Sun protection – sun glasses, head cover and sunscreen lotion should always be in your beach bag.

Safety on Trails

Hike, bike or run with a companion if possible, if you are active in the back country. At least leave detailed information on your planned route.

Maps are always good for orientation and fun to work with. Your footwear should be appropriate to trail conditions.

Your backpack should hold an extra T-shirt, sun protection and a rain jacket (in winter).

A cell phone or at least a whistle can become a life saving device once you are lost or injured.

Sufficient fluids are mandatory, especially in summer.

There are mountain lions in the back country of Orange County. However, they rarely approach humans; they hardly ever contact groups, and they do not like noise. Keep children close to adults while hiking in the back country.

Using a map can be helpful

You might also encounter snakes in the wilderness. Most of them are harmless. It is fun to watch them, but keep a safe distance and also stay on trails to avoid rattle snakes.

Poisonous oak is common in Orange County. Educate yourself in how it looks, and again, staying on trails will save you trouble.

For any kind of biking or inline skating wear a helmet, for inline skating we additionally recommend wearing wrist and knee protection.

Getting Around in Orange County

Poison Oak in fall

The residents of Orange County are car addicted. So, expect to find cars in motion all day and night.

Expressways are constantly being "improved", and even though you will find more than twenty lanes e.g. at El Toro Y at the widest point, where Interstate 5 and 405 meet, at busy times traffic jams are abundant.

Highway 1 (Pacific Coast Highway or just PCH) runs all the way North to South through the Beach Cities of Orange County.

However, all the way through Laguna Beach Highway 1 is a nightmare to the driver on weekends and holidays. Either come with patience, or in case you stay or live in the vicinity of Laguna's beaches, walk, bike or take the city bus.

Bike to your activity site

Buses, run by the Orange County Transportation Authority, in general are an excellent choice in Orange County. From inland cities they go to most beach cities. We can strongly recommend Route 1, since you can travel on it the entire coastline from Long Beach to San Clemente for a minimal fee.

Presently it costs less than two dollars for a local ride in Orange County. Up to three children six and under are free with an adult.

For seniors or disabled persons there is a discount. You can also get day passes as well as weekly and monthly passes. Buses go about every half an hour during busy times, otherwise about every hour..

A train in San Clemente

3. Activities in Coastal Areas

Surfing near the pier, Huntington Beach

General Area Huntington Beach

→ Huntington Beach – Coastline
→ Huntington Harbor
→ Huntington Beach City Parks
→ Other Activity Sites in the Area

www.ci-Huntington-Beach.ca.us
www.ci.costa-mesa.ca.us
www.fountainvalley.org

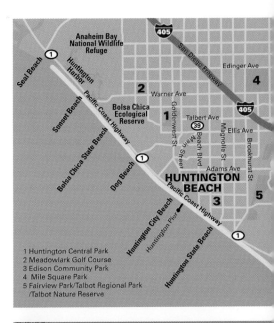

1 Huntington Central Park
2 Meadowlark Golf Course
3 Edison Community Park
4 Mile Square Park
5 Fairview Park/Talbot Regional Park
/Talbot Nature Reserve

Orientation:

Huntington Beach (HB), one of northern Orange County's beach cities lacks the bluffs and hills further south, because of the city's location within the Los Angeles Basin. However, it offers 8.5 miles of uninterrupted sandy beachfront and includes a pier stretching out nearly two thousand feet into the ocean.

HB is also known as Surf City, since surfing legend Duke Kahamanamoku started a surfing vibe here, which is still going strong today.

Huntington Harbor (HH) is lined by mansions of various architectural styles. It is sought after by boaters especially on weekends. Opposite HH on the coast lies unincorporated Sunset Beach.

If you are looking for activities inland, especially more formal activities, go to Huntington Central Park, covering over 450 acres. It stands out from the 60 plus city parks for the many activities it offers, including horseback riding and frisbee golf.

Fairview Park and Talbot Regional Park a few blocks inland from the ocean in neighboring Costa Mesa offer what Huntington Beach lacks: bluffs. They provide challenging courses to the BMX bike rider, as well as many trails to

Huntington City Beach north of the pier

the walker, jogger, biker and horse back rider. 640-acre Mile Square Park in neighboring Fountain Valley is another green oasis in the urban setting, which is a favorite of bike riders, hikers and formal sports enthusiasts like golfers or tennis players.

Huntington Beach – Coastline

→ Bolsa Chica State Beach
→ Huntington City Beach
→ Huntington State Beach

Rating: ●●●●◖

Best Time: All year, but even better in late spring, summer, and fall.

Location: From the Santa Ana river mouth in the south to the end of Huntington Harbor and the community of Sunset Beach in the north along Pacific Coast Highway (PCH).

Access: Easy. You can't miss the beaches if you go up or down Pacific Coast Highway. Park either directly on PCH (metered parking, you need a lot of quarters), or in the gated parking areas of the state beaches, or to the south and and north of HB pier, where in the north you pay a daily fee, and in the south you have metered parking.

If you don't mind walking a little you can park free in neighboring streets in the vicinity of the beaches. (Come early during summer months.) At Huntington State Beach near Magnolia entrance, there are even beach wheelchairs available for those who want to get beyond the paved ramps that lead towards the beach.

Profile of the Beaches: The beaches are divided in three areas.

Bolsa Chica State Beach to the north and Huntington State Beach to the south are managed by the California Department of Parks and Recreation. The beach area north and south of the pier and Dog Beach a little further north are managed by the City of Huntington Beach. Other than slightly different parking fees, and minor differences in surfing hours, all three are very similar. If you prefer to be where the action is, settle near the pier, at the extension of busy Main Street. If you want more space try the southern or northern areas of the beaches.

There is one setback though to the beauty of the

Beach life, Central Huntington Beach

extensive white sands and the glistening waters of the Pacific in Huntington Beach.

The active oilfield inland in the north, the fuming stacks of a power plant in the south and the results of the never ending development in between reduce the pleasure.

You can forget it, if you keep your face turned seawards, while going down Pacific Coast Highway along the beaches.

Otherwise, the beaches are truly outstanding: sandy and one of the widest in California (in average about a hundred yards wide); they offer a family style atmosphere.

Facilities: All three beach areas offer drinking fountains, cold-water showers, restrooms, wheelchair accessible ramps and restrooms, firerings (about 600), RVcamping is fashionable at the two State Beaches (No tents though).

Special Features: Great news for dog owners! Dog Beach north of the pier between Seapoint Avenue and Golden West Street is one of the few off-leash dog beaches in Southern California.

Other Attractions: Bolsa Chica Ecological Reserve covers 1700 acres of coastal wetlands on the east side of PCH, opposite Bolsa Chica State Beach between Warner and Seapoint Avenue. Hundreds of migrating birds spend the winter at the wetlands.

Huntington Beach Pier, one of the longest Piers in California (1853feet), invites many visitors to a leisurely stroll. You can also try your luck in fishing, since it is free.

Where the pier starts, at Pier Plaza, there are frequent summer concerts and a weekly market. Near the pier watch out for the bronze bust of Duke Kahamanamoku, the multiple Olympic swim champion from Hawaii, who introduced 1911 surfing here when visiting on his way to the 1912 Olympics in Stockholm.

The boards at that time were made out of redwood, were ten feet long and weighed 135 pounds.

International Surfing Museum (411 Olive Avenue) is proof that it all started in Huntington Beach.

Dog Beach north of Huntington Pier

Bolsa Chica Ecological Reserve

Huntington Beach Pier

Waiting for the big wave

For The Hungy and Thirsty: For a lunch at the City Beach, try Sandy's at the beach on the base of the pier, or Duke´s Huntigton Beach (the name honors surfing legend Duke) on the upper level in the building, both with patios facing the volleyball courts, the pier and the Pacific Ocean. If you fall for a view, Ruby's at the end of the pier is a choice.

The Longboard (217 Main Street), is the oldest restaurant in HB, and is located in the oldest building in town, offering two outdoor patios. There are concession stands at each entrance to Huntington State Beach.

■ Water Activities

Swimming, Surfing, Boogie Boarding, Boating

In summer, on holidays and during the weekend beaches are crowded, especially in the vicinity of the pier. Water temperatures in summer are 66 to 70 degrees. In winter the Pacific can be chilly, 55 to 61 degrees, and temperatures by the water are considerably cooler than further inland. Also consider the wind chill factor. However, winter months are best for surfing.

Swimming: You will find consistent surf breaks, and no rocks on the sandy ocean floor.

Also, the waves break rather far from the shore line, which creates shallow waters near the shore, ideal for swimming and bathing, especially for families with children.

Skimboarding

If you swim out in the ocean, stay near staffed lifeguard towers, and avoid swimming alone.

In case you want to avoid crowds, venture quite a bit south on Huntington State Beach, (where you will easily find lots of space and much less noise).

Surfing: Huntington Beach has its name Surf City for a reason, since you can find surfers here almost all hours of the day year around.

The US Open of Surfing, the biggest surfing event in the world, is held at HB and the USA Surf Team practices here. Different from other places, where surfing is prohibited during peak hours, here most areas are permanently open to surfing, with few restrictions in summer.

Bolsa Chica State Beach, in the north of Surf City is best for beginners and less experienced surfers, since surf is known to be gentle here.

As a more adventorous surfer you can join the experts along the pier. But watch out. Surfers can be very territorial.

Boogie Boarding: This is the easiest way to ride waves (perfect for novice surfers that lack the technique to ride a surf board). It is getting more and more popular all over the place especially at the northern parts of Huntington Beach.

Boating: You can launch a man-powered boat at any of the beaches. Note however, that you will have to carry your boat quite a way through the sands, before you can launch it here.

■ Trail Activities

Walking, Hiking, Jogging, Running, Biking, Inline Skating

A paved pathway, the Huntington Beach Ocean Strand, runs from the Santa Anna river mouth at the border to Newport Beach for eight and a half miles along the HB beaches. It is very inviting for all kinds of trail activities, since you can be active and at the same time enjoy the

Huntington Beach Ocean Strand - a paradise for trail activities

vista of the ocean. Walkers and hikers share the path with cyclists, joggers, inline skaters and skate boarders.

Trip: **Along the Boardwalk at PCH**
Inline Skating, Biking

Rating: ●●●●◐
Best Time: All year, crowded on weekends, during weekday mornings rather empty.
For cyclists that like some speed, this tour is best on weekdays from morning till afternoon.
Difficulty: Easy, zero elevation gain.
Distance: From four miles (just to the pier) to 8.5 miles (to the end of the boardwalk) to ten miles (including Bolsa Chica Reserve).
Special Features: The Orange County Transportation Authority (OCTA) provides buses with bike racks to almost all places you want to start or finish your activity. Therefore, if you just want to go one-way, the bus will bring your back to your car.
The Trip: You can choose your starting point: either start out at the Santa Anna river mouth and go north, or you begin your activity in the north at Huntington Harbor and go south. You can also make Bolsa Chica Ecological Reserve you trailhead.

Where you turn or end is your choice. The pier at HB is a good destination for walkers, hikers and moderate joggers; it's a good turning point for runners. It invites cyclists and inline skaters for a stopover and a stroll out on the pier before they go on to the southern or northern end.
From Santa Anna River mouth: From PCH, turn into Orange Street in north NB just south of the Santa Ana River, then immediately right on Seashore Drive, where you can park free or use your quarters in the metered parking lot.
Walk up to PCH, either through the metered parking lot there, which has a pedestrian access to PCH, or by walking up the stairs at the end of Seashore. Turn north on PCH, cross the Santa Ana River bridge, enter the Ocean Strand and start you activity.
From Huntington Harbor: Coming from PCH, turn inland at the southern end of HH just before the intersection with Warner Avenue next to the fire station and near the HH Yacht Club. There you can park (free).
From Bolsa Chica Ecological Reserve: Coming from PCH turn into the reserve parking lot just opposite from the entrance to Bolsa Chica State Beach (free for visitors).
If you start at the Santa Ana River mouth, make your way back from your parking spot to PCH,

Skating along Ocean Strand near the pier

Running at the water's edge

Volleyball courts south of the pier in Huntungton Beach

cross the Santa Ana bridge and enter the bicycle path that runs along the beach. Follow it and enjoy the vista: Catalina Island to the left, Huntington Pier ahead and San Pedro and Redondo Beach in the distance. Don't look right though, since the giant power plant might spoil your pristine beach experience.

The surface of the path is in good shape There are no major bumps and hardly any inclines or descents. Going towards the pier, you will likely face headwinds, which makes skating or running back such a pleasure, as the wind gives you an easy time.

Modification: Walk, or jog part of the trip through the sand along the ocean, especially in the south (Huntington State Beach) or in the city (Huntington City Beach), which not only keeps you away from the noisy PCH, but also makes it easier on your joints.

Formal Sports Activities

Beach Volleyball

Rating: ●●●●●
Best Time: All year, even in summer there is hardly any waiting time.
Location: Most nets are up south and north of the Pier, and also at the Newland and Beach Boulevard entrance.

There are close to thirty sand volleyball courts at the beach. They are a heaven for leisurely players as well as for intense competitors. Volleyball professionals hold a tournament here once a year.

Most nets are up all year, and you play on a first-come first-serve basis. Activities are going on every day; one can easily find a group to join. If you don't have a ball, you can rent one at the concession stands.

Huntington Harbor from Peter's Landing

Huntington Harbor (HH)

Location: In the northwest corner of Huntington Beach on the inland side of PCH between Warner Avenue in the south and Edinger Avenue in the north.

Access: Since the harbor almost borders Pacific Coast Highway it is easy to find. Access to the water, however, is another matter. You can park in most streets on the islands or on the west side of the harbor, but unlike Newport Beach, there are no public walkways around the islands. Access to the water is possible at very few tiny public beaches and two public boat ramps. If you get your boat at one of the boat rentals on PCH at the harbor a couple of blocks north of Warner Avenue, your can start your journey right there.

Profile: All kinds of boaters enjoy the calm waters of Huntington Harbor with its five man-made public islands. The harbor connects with the Pacific Ocean via the Anaheim Bay. All channels between the islands are navigable, however some are rather narrow.

Facilities: No public facilities.

For the Hungry and Thirsty: There are eateries along PCH. Try some at Peter's Landing, either Chinese food at Panda's Palace, or Vietnamese food at small An's restaurant, both off 16400 Pacific Coast Highway.

■ Water Activities

Boating

The Trips: Around the Islands in HH

Rating: ●●●●
Best Time: All year.

Ocean kayaks

You can launch your own kayak or canoe at any of the small harbor beaches. The most convenient public launch ramp though is on Warner Avenue near the intersection with PCH in the vicinity of the Huntington Harbor Yacht Club and next to the fire station.

If you rent a kayak or a canoe a little further north at Peter's Landing or Sunset Yacht Rentals on the harbor side, you can launch it there.

It's great fun to navigate your boat through the channels between the islands, and to admire the yachts and the mansions onshore.

Always stay to your right, and avoid coming too close to larger vessels.

You can also launch your kayak from charming little Seabridge Park in the north of Huntington Harbor near the end of Edinger on Countess Avenue (free parking). Also, restrooms and showers are provided. Tiny Mother's Beach right at the bridge to Humboldt Island is another alternative for launching; no facilities though.

Trip 1: Turn inland from the public launching ramp, then turn left (north) after you pass Davenport Island. Go under Davenport Bridge; keep going north, pass Humboldt Island and go under Humboldt Bridge. Take a left turn at the end of Humboldt Island and circle Trinidad first on its north side, passing under Trinidad Bridge. Turn south and pass Gilbert Island on your right; continue south to your starting point.

Depending on your paddling experience, this trip can take up to two hours.

Modification 1: You can also launch your boat

Kayaking in the harbor

Mother's Beach in Huntington Harbor

from Mother's Beach at the entrance to Humboldt Island; go north from there and follow the above tour.

Modification 2: If you want just an hour's exercise, start out as in trip 1, pass Davenport Island, circle Humboldt Island all the way and continue south to your starting point.

Trip 2: If you launch your boat at Sunset Yacht Rentals you can turn left and paddle north along Admiralty Island, then cross the main channel, and continue north of Trinidad Island. Pass under the Trinidad bridge, at the end of the island turn left and soon thereafter right. Circle Humboldt Island. Either take the big trip and circle Davenport Island or take the shortcut north of Davenport Island. Turn north after you reach the main channel. Once you reach Gilbert Island turn left and continue to your starting point on the south side of Gilbert Island.

The big trip will last about two hours, taking the short cut you finish half an hour earlier.

Snowy egrets, Huntington Harbour

Exercising on World Trail in Huntington Central Park

Huntington Beach City Parks and Other Sports Facilities
→ Huntington Central Park
→ More Formal Activities at Other Sites

Rating: ●●●●
Location: On both sides of Golden West Street between Ellis Avenue and Slater Avenue, about two miles inland from PCH and the ocean.
Access: Access is possible at several areas. The parking lot by the library off Golden West Street at Talbert Avenue provides free parking. So does the parking lot at Park Bench Café about a hundred yards further inland on Golden West Street, in case you choose the eastern side of the park, near Lake Talbert as the starting point for your activity.

If you are heading for the disc golf course, there is a special parking area, off Golden West Street, just north of Ellis Avenue (free).
At the Equestrian Center further north off

Huntington Central Park Sports Park

Golden West Street, parking is also free.
In case Lake Huntingon is your starting point,
take Ellis Avenue off Golden West Street to
Edwards Avenue and then turn right on Inlet
Drive or Central Park Drive, which both end at
the park, where you can park free or you can use
the parking lot of Alice's Breakfast in the Park,
if you plan on eating there after your activity.
Last not least, there is a huge parking lot right at
the sports complex (fee).

Profile: Huntington Central Park stands out
from over sixty city parks. The 354 acre
property is one of the region's largest
greenbelts, divided by Golden West Street. Six
miles of paved trails and a few miles of dirt
trails meander through Central Park.
Central Park East features a rather new sports
complex, including seven baseball fields and as
many soccer fields, and several batting cages.
An exercise par course (World Trail) around
Lake Talbert invites to be active.
Ther is also a grass volleyball court.
Central Park West offers the Disc Golf Course,
the Huntington Central Park Equestrian Center,
and a dog park.

Facilities: Restrooms at the restaurants and the
library, drinking fountains, a great adventure
playground at Central Park East.
For the Hungry and Thirsty: Park Bench Cafe
on Golden West Street in Central Park East has
outdoor seating and even serves food for dogs.

■ Trail Activities
Walking, Jogging, Horseback Riding

Trip: Around the Lakes in Huntington
Central Park
Walking, Running
Rating: ●●●●
Best Time: Spring
Distance: Up to three miles.
Difficulty: Easy
Access to Starting Point: From Pacific Coast
Highway turn inland on Golden West Street.
Once you cross Ellis Avenue you see the park

Riding at the Equestrian Center

Park Bench Café in Central Park

to your left and your right. Turn right into the
parking lot of Park Bench Café after you pass
the Huntington Library to your right. You can
also park in the parking lot of the library, and
walk a few steps over to Lake Talbert and the
Café. If you park in the first huge parking lot to
your right, which connects to the Sports
Complex, you have to pay a fee.

Profile: You will circle both of the lakes on
mostly paved path, with no elevation gains.

The Trip: Start out at the Park Bench Café.
Circle Talbert Lake in either direction on the
World Trail (marked, 1.2 miles), do the
suggested exercises, if you like, then cross
Golden West Street, follow the street for about
100 yards. Then take the trail to your right and
keep left at each intersection until you reach
Huntington Lake; circle it, and return via the
same route to Golden West Street and the

parking lot at Park Bench Café. Runners can extend their activity up to five miles, if they keep to the right (north, northwest) and jog through Shipley Nature Center and enjoy part of the 18 acre preserve, before turning left towards Huntington Lake.

Horseback Riding at Central Park Equestrian Center
Rating: ●●●●

Location/Access: The Equestrian Center is located right on Golden West Street just north of Ellis Avenue; you will see it from the street.

Profile: The 25 acre Equestrian Center in Huntington Central Park East is another attraction of HB. All styles of riding are offered, from jumpers and dressage to western style and trail riding. You can enjoy riding in a scenic setting of 185 acres of trails. It even features a Therapeutic Riding Center.

One hour guided trail rides into the hills overlooking Central Park and the Pacific Ocean are offered for all ability levels (walking only).

Equestrian Center, Huntington Beach

▇ Formal Sports Activities at Central Park and Other Sites

Frisbee-Golf, Volleyball, Soccer, Baseball, Skateboarding, Tennis, Golf, Basketball, Handball

Frisbee-Golf
Rating: ●●●●◖

Best time: All year.

Location/Access: At Golden West Street across from Central Library, close to Ellis Avenue. They have a large parking lot.

Profile: If you are looking for moderate exercise, then Frisbee-golf is the sport for you. Huntington Beach offers a world-class setting for this rather new sport combining golf and frisbee. It is played like golf with a disc instead of a golf ball which you throw into a basket. Huntington Beach Central Park offers an 18 target course which covers over 600 yards. It opened thirty years ago, and is one of the nicest

Frisbee-Golf area, Huntington Central Park

courses of its kind in California.

Over 4000 players come each month, with a growing number of expert tournament players. But it is also a family activity, where kids can join in (small fee). The Pro Shop rents discs.

Facilities: Portable restrooms available.

Volleyball: There are some grass volleyball courts in Huntington Central Park West.

Other: The rather new Huntington Central Park Sports Complex has plenty of soccer and baseball fields, as well as batting cages. However, they are mostly used for team competitions, and you will have to rent and reserve them.

Skateboarding
Rating: ●●●●◖ on public boardwalks, ●●● in parks
Best time: All year.
In Huntington Beach skateboarding is so popular that many consider it a way of moving through town. However, in some areas of Huntington Beach skateboarding is illegal. On Main Street and on downtown sidewalks skateboarding is not permitted.

Tennis in Huntington Beach

Lighted basketball fields at Edison Park

There are three small free public skateboard parks in Huntington Beach.
Location/Access: Huntington Beach Skate Park: At 1902 Main Street by HB High School. Drive close to two miles inland from the pier. You find the tiny park on left side of the Main Street before Yorktown intersection.
Murdy Skate Park is at 7000 Norma Drive between Warner and Heil Avenue.
Oak View Center Park you find at 17261 Oak Lane close to Warner Avenue.

Tennis
Rating: ●●●●
Best Time: All year.
There are 72 tennis courts open to the public in Surf City. However, the majority of them are not located in attractive parks. In the following we just list two sites with lighted courts.
Location/Access: At Golden West College at 115744 Golden West Street you find six lighted hard courts (open until 8.30pm), where you have to be aware of classes during the week, but otherwise hardly ever have to wait.
The four courts at forty acre Edison Community Park at 21377 Magnolia Street in the south of Huntington Beach a few blocks from the ocean are surrounded by paved paths winding through grassy open area and are also part of the parks various sport facilities.
Basketball: Several lighted basketball courts at Edison Community Park at 21377 Magnolia Street.
Handball: Courts at Edison Community Park.

Golf
Rating: ●●●●
Best Time: All year.
Huntington Beach had one of the oldest Golf Courses in Orange County. Meadowlark Golf Club at Graham Street near Warner Avenue is open to the public.
Location/Access: Meadowlark Golf Club is on 16782 Graham Street between Warner Avenue and Heil Avenue. Go inland on Warner

Meadowlark Golf Course

Avenue in North Huntington Beach for about one and a half mile, turn left on Graham Street. **Profile:** 18 hole course. Lighted driving range, chipping, and putting green allow for evening practice. Discount prices for evening play, on weekdays and for seniors.

Other Activity Sites in the Area

➜ Fairview Park, Talbert Nature Preserve
➜ Talbert Regional Park
➜ Miles Square Regional Park

Fairview Park, Talbert Nature Preserve
Rating: ●●●●◖
Best time: Year round.
Location: 2525 Placentia Avenue, Costa Mesa.
Access: From the 405 Freeway exit Harbor Boulevard. Go south on Harbor Boulevard, turn right on Wilson Drive and then right on

Placentia Avenue. After you pass Estancia High School turn left into parking area.
Profile: Fairview Park is unique as it offers a great spectrum of opportunities for outdoor activities in varied natural settings. Hikers, bikers, runners and horseback riders can enjoy the circling and criss-crossing trails. Dogs kept on a leash are welcome too.
The park lies adjacent to the Santa Ana Bicycle Trail which connects it to Talbert Regional Park The park also displays interesting geographical features with a plateau area, bluffs and a riparian area close to the river below the bluffs. Wildlife and indigenous vegetation can be found in six separate zones based on plant groups found along the Santa Ana River. These plant areas include Coastal Strand, Native Grassland, Alluvial Woodland, and more.
Well maintained nature trails are ideal for

Fairview Park in nearby Costa Mesa

A challenging bike route in Fairview Park

joggers and horseback riders. Bumpy paths on the plateau, and the bluffs for the most daring, invite bike riders.

Facilities: Restrooms, drinking fountains, picnic areas.

For the Hungry and Thirsty: Bring your own provisions and enjoy in one of the picnic areas.

■ Trail Activities

Walking, Hiking, Jogging, Biking,

Trip 1: Circle Talbert Nature Preserve
Walking, Jogging
Rating: ●●●●◖
Distance: Three miles.
Difficulty: Easy
Best Time: Morning hours, cool season.
Access: From the parking area, turn right on the paved trail and descend to the lower section.

The Trip: Turn left into the Talbert Nature Preserve Area onto an unpaved trail. Follow the trail until it ends in the Santa Ana Bike Trail; return and turn left passing through the first fence gate on your left, continuing on a different nature trail.

When you reach the fence paralleling the Santa Ana Bike Trail turn right. Follow it. It will veer to the right where you reach the turn-off point and the paved trail, which takes you back uphill to the parking area.

Modification 1: (Three additional miles). Instead of turning around at the end, continue on the Santa Ana Bike Trail, cross Victoria Street/Hamilton Avenue and enter Talbert Regional Park on a small dirt path (unsigned). Now you can extend your activity for several more miles incorporating many unpaved trails of the park. Return to Fairview Park.

Modification 2: (additional miles) Instead of entering Talbert Regional Park continue on the

Biking in spring, Talbert Nature Preserve

Stretching in Talbert Park, Costa Mesa

bike trail by crossing Victoria Street/Hamilton Avenue taking the underpass. When you reach the bike trail that parallels Pacific Coast Highway, you either turn left to Newport Beach or right to Huntington Beach.

Talbert Regional Park
Rating: ●●●●
Best time: Year round.
Location: 1298 Victoria Street, Costa Mesa
Access: From Talbert Nature Preserve access is as described in Trip 1 of Fairview Park. Another access point is from Santa Ana Bicycle Trail half a mile south of Victoria Street.
The park has also many access trails from the

surrounding neighborhoods. Come by bike or park in the streets and walk.
Profile: Talbert Regional Park is the continuation of Talbert Nature Preserve south of Victoria Street.
Tidal gates have been installed into the eastern river channel wall allowing water to flow in and out of the park, creating a large pond and wetlands. Many dirt trails lead through the park and are often shaded by large riparian vegetation.
Special Features: This park is a favorite for BMX bikers for whom Riding Parks within the park have been constructed. The 'Kiddy Rack' is for the youngsters, followed by 'Sheep Hills' which gives Talbert Regional Park its second name, and then by 'Styles' for the experts.

Mile Square Regional Park
with Recreation Center and Sports Park
Rating: ●●●●
Best Time: Any time.
Location: 16801 Euclid Street, Fountain Valley.
Access: Take the Interstate 405. Exit at the Euclid Street/Newhope Street exit. Turn onto Euclid Street going north. Cross Warner Avenue and turn left into the main park entrance (fee).

Talbert Lake, Costa Mesa

Archery at Mile Square Park, Fountain Valley

Profile: This urban park feels huge! The trail system within is attractive for jogging, rollerblading, walking and biking. Also, a bikeway is circumventing the park.

There are two lakes in the park which are open for fishing and paddle boat use. Within the North Lake lies Palm Island with beautiful flowers, a gazebo and many benches.

Also in the northern a nature area offfers native plants and a butterfly garden.

Facilities: Restrooms, barbecues, fire rings, picnic areas, playgrounds.

Special Features: A recent addition is One-Night-Stay Camping Facility for youth groups.

For the Hungry and Thirsty: Plenty of trees providing shade for a picnic; also covered shelters; concession stands.

■ Trail Activities

Walking, Jogging, Bicycling, Inline Skating

Trip: Criss-Cross Mile Square
Regional Park
Biking, Walking, Inline Skating

Rating: ●●●●
Distance: Four miles circling the park, about three miles inside the park.
Difficulty: Easy
Best Time: Any time when surface is dry.
The Trip: Enter the park at the main entrance off Euclid Street and park (fee). During a weekday morning, you can also park along Edinger Avenue (free) and start from there.
Work your way to the perimeter of the park and

Family outing in Mile Square Park

start your tour around the park on the bikeway and/or walkway. The pavement is mostly in good shape. Watch out for traffic coming out of the parking lots, along Warner Avenue where you pass Mile Square Golf Course.

Also watch out along Brookhurst Avenue where you pass the Boys and Girls Club, the Fountain Valley Community Center and the Tennis Center, along Edinger Avenue, where you pass a park entry and then along Euclid where you pass several park exits before you come back to the main entry.

Or, you stay within the park and choose the trails you like. All are in great condition and you cannot get lost.

■ Formal Sports Activities
Golf, Archery, Other

Golf: Two golf courses lie within the park boundaries.

Mile Square Golf Course, in the southwestern part, located at 10401 Warner Avenue, offers two challenging regulation 18 hole courses,

'The Player' and 'The Classic.' A driving range and a coffee shop with a bar complete the facility. Mile Square Golf Course has been consistently rated as one of the three best golf courses in Orange County. For that, it is reasonably priced; but there are less expensive courses in Orange County.

On the north side lies David L. Baker Golf Course at 10410 Edinger Avenue. It offers an executive length 18 hole course complete with driving range, where you can aim at a large truck, and practice bunker. The course is very family friendly and is reasonably priced, but the least expensive T-time still costs 20 dollars plus.

Archery: An outdoor archery range is available to the public by reservation.

Other: Three softball fields, two baseball fields, two soccer fields, and two lakes with paddle boat rental exist within the park boundaries. Also bicycle rental is available with a great variety of bikes.

Fountain Valley Recreation Center and Sports Park
Rating: ●●●●◖
Best time: Any time.
Location: 16400 Brookhurst Street, Fountain Valley.
Access: From Interstate 405 exit at Brookhurst Street and go north. At Heil Avenue, turn right.

David L. Baker Golf Course

Fountain Valley Tennis Center in Mile Square Park

You will see a large sign Fountain Valley Recreation Center and Sports Park.

Profile: The Recreation Center lies within the block of Mile Square Park adjacent to the Golf courses and the park area. The center was just recently expanded and improved. Even though it is mostly geared to more formal sports activities, it also features a network of paved and nature trails that connect to the trails of Mile Square Regional Park.

Facilities: Restrooms, large picnic area with an outdoor stage, playground, picnic tables, benches, water fountains.

For the Hungry and Thirsty: Bring supplies for a picnic, or get them at the concession stand.

Fun on the greens in Mile Square Park

■ Formal Sports Activities

Tennis, Basketball, Others

Tennis: Twelve lighted tennis courts and two half courts at Fountain Valley Tennis Center (fee). Mostly occupied with courses, but courts can also be reserved through the city (fee). It seems to be a little expensive in an area where use of courts usually is free, but on Sunday afternoon the courts are open to family play (free).

Basketball: Six lighted basketball courts.

Other: Three handball courts, fifteen ball fields.

Harbor View Park near famous surfing spot The Wedge

General Area Newport Beach

→ Balboa Peninsula
→ Newport Harbor
→ Corona del Mar State Beach
→ Little Corona Beach
→ Upper Back Bay
→ Newport Beach City Parks and
   Recreational Facilities

www.newportbeachca.gov
vwww.ocparks.org

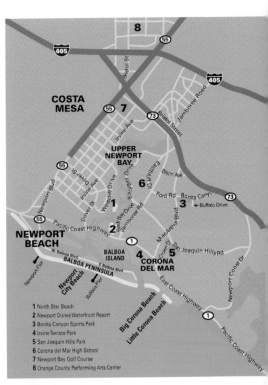

1 North Star Beach
2 Newport Dunes Waterfront Resort
3 Bonita Canyon Sports Park
4 Irvine Terrace Park
5 San Joaquin Hills Park
6 Corona del Mar High School
7 Newport Bay Golf Course
8 Orange County Performing Arts Center

Orientation:

Newport Beach has got it all. Opportunities for actively enjoying the aquatic world are almost unlimited. Scenic trails invite you for activities on foot, on wheels or on horses.

There are three great beaches within the city limits:

Newport Beach Municipal Beach stretches from the Santa Ana River Jetty through Newport and Balboa Piers on Balboa Peninsula up to the famous Wedge by the north jetty of the harbor mouth; it is by far the largest of the three city beach areas.

Corona del Mar State Beach – also known as Big Corona Beach in the community of Corona del Mar is the city's family beach, in summer crowded by residents and visitors alike.

Little Corona Beach is a marvel of a cove beach framed by rocky bluffs in Corona del Mar. Local families love it, so do scuba divers.

Newport Harbor with its seven man-made islands and over 9000 boats also has beaches, but it should be explored by boat.

Sunset on the pier in Balboa Peninsula

Back Bay view from Aquatic Center at North Star Beach

Famous Back Bay is another jewel for the outdoor activist. The trails around Back Bay permits you to discover it on foot, on bikes on inline skates, or even on horseback.

It offers two beach areas: Newport Dunes Waterfront Resort is privately owned, but open to the public. It covers over a mile of sandy shore. North Star Beach, is home to the Newport Aquatic Center, a non-profit organization. It is the door to Upper Bay Ecological Reserve one of the few estuaries left in California, best to be explored by boat.

The over forty City Parks and recreational facilities of Newport Beach are very well kept, and invite to more formal sports activities such as baseball, basketball, soccer, tennis, lap swimming, track and field, and lawn bowling.

The greatest nearby cultural attraction is Orange County Performing Arts Center. Venues include Segerstrom Hall, the Renee and Henry Segerstrom Concert Hall and the South Coast Repertory Theater, all located at 600 Town Center Drive in Costa Mesa very close to the city limits of Newport Beach. They are easily reached from the 405 or 55 Freeways. You can

Segerstrom Hall at the Performing Arts Center, Costa Mesa

Famous Dory Fishing Fleet

Balboa Peninsula – Newport Beach Municipal Beach

Rating: ●●●●●
Best Time: All year, but even better in late spring, summer and fall.
Location: Balboa Peninsula in Newport Beach off Pacific Coast Highway via Newport Boulevard.
Access: In north Newport Beach turn off Pacific Coast Highway on West Balboa Boulevard, which runs the length of Balboa Peninsula. Drive down the boulevard, turn right at 21st Street and park at the city parking lot (fee) at Newport Pier, or proceed to Main Street, turn right and park at the city parking lot at the Balboa Pier (fee). Parking is free in the side streets, however, one morning per week, street cleaning prohibits parking.
Profile: The original sand pit created by the Santa Ana River has become the center of the beach activities in Newport Beach year round. From the Santa Ana River Jetty through Newport and Balboa Piers sparkling golden sand stretches over six miles up to 250 feet deep along the coast. It ends at the world famous surfing spot, The Wedge, by the north jetty at the harbor mouth and Harbor View Park.

enjoy world class performances. The architecture alone is definitively worth a visit. Newport Beach also houses the Orange County Art Museum at 850 San Clemente Drive.

The ferry connects Balboa Peninsula to Balboa Island

Enjoying the daring surfers

At a scenic boardwalk, open to all kinds of activities, luxurious mansions line the sands.

Near the piers the beach is very crowded in summer, on weekends and on holidays.

That's where the action is. If you look for some quiet spots you can find them between 11th and 9th Street north of Balboa Pier and between I and L Streets south of it.

Facilities at the Peninsula: Restrooms, showers, drinking fountains, fire rings (Balboa Pier), at the piers and on 12th Street. There are no facilities at the West Jetty View Park.

Other Attractions: Since Newport Beach's modern history started on Balboa Peninsula, you find landmarks like the Balboa Pavilion here.

Local history is also evident with the Dory Fishing Fleet, just north of Newport Pier. Since 1880 they have launched their wooden dories from this spot. It is the last of its kind in the US.

Sometimes, if you come for fresh fish at eight in the morning, they are already sold out.

Try the tiny Balboa Island Ferry (three cars only) which crosses the harbor all day from Palm Street near Balboa Pier to Balboa Island and admire yachts and mansions at the harbor.

The Catalina Flyer which serves to Catalina Island some forty-five miles out in the Pacific, starts from Balboa Pavilion every morning and returns in the late afternoon.

For the Hungry and Thirsty: Eateries are all over the place near the piers.

The Crab Cooker is a unique seafood place close to Newport Pier. If you prefer a great view, you can lunch at a restaurant either at the end of Balboa Pier, or of Newport Pier.

At the tiny Stuft Surfer Café directly on the boardwalk at the corner of 15th street you sit under some palms outdoors by the sand.

Spectacular surfing at The Wedge

■ Water Activities

Swimming, Surfing, Bodyboarding,
Bodysurfing, Scuba Diving, Snorkeling,
SUP, Boating

Swimming: The beach north of Balboa Pier up to Newport Pier is level, where the water meets the sand. Therefore, this is the area for families with children. South of Balboa Pier the ocean floor descends steeply, where it meets the water, causing the surf to smash down on the sand, making it unsafe for inexperienced swimmers. It is even worse at The Wedge, where the surf can rise up to twenty feet. No swimmers here, only expert (body) surfers!

Water quality is mostly A. Check the local papers for daily ratings.

Surfing, Bodyboarding, and Bodysurfing: The beaches on Balboa Peninsula mostly suit the average surfer, since you can surf at swells from all directions, and the bottoms are sandy. There is one outstanding area though: The Wedge. It is by some considered one of the toughest bodysurfing spot in the US. Waves and reflected waves can meet following waves, thus creating peaks which a few times in a year will go up to 20 feet and draw only the most daring experts and hundreds of spectators.

Since the waves break right at the sand, the wedge is a rather dangerous place, and accidents happen. It is recommended mostly for short-boards.

There is another spot for experienced surfers though: the Santa Ana river jetties at the very north end of the municipal beaches right at the boarder to Huntington Beach. The effects of the breaking waves are similar here to those at The Wedge but not quite as demanding.

Scuba Diving and Snorkeling: Of no significance at Balboa Peninsula beaches,

Walking along Balboa Peninsula

except for one spot at low tide: the Newport Pier, since it extends to the edge of the Newport submarine canyon. However, this is for experts, since diving under piers can be dangerous, and visibility is often poor here. The condition can improve in fall, if the Santa Ana winds blow the surface water out and thus clean up the area.

Stand-Up-Paddeling: The new sport of stand-up-paddeling (SUP) is catching on in Newport Beach too. It is easiest in the harbor or on Back Bay; advanced paddlers do it on the Pacific.

Boating: Though it is permitted to launch a hand carried boat from the beaches, it is more convenient to start your kayak trips from the harbor or from Back Bay, if you don't live right at the water's edge.

The best place on Balboa Peninsula for launching your kayak in the ocean seems to be at Newport Pier, since the parking lot is close and the shore breaks are smallish most often.

■ Trail Activities

Walking, Running, Biking, Inline Skating

A very scenic paved boardwalk runs along most of the peninsula (from 36th street in the north to F Street in the south), inviting active people year round.

Walking: Since the beaches at Balboa peninsula are nowhere fenced in you have access to the beach from all the little side streets and you can start your trip anywhere.

Trip: Balboa Pier to The Wedge
Walking

Rating: ●●●●●
Distance: Two and a half miles, six miles, if you start at Newport Pier.
Difficulty: Easy
Best Time: All year, except busy summer days and weekends, supreme on weekday mornings.
The Walk: Start at the Balboa Pier, after parking in one of the side streets; use the boardwalk up to F street. Continue your walk to the Wedge directly on the shore in the sand, watching out for migrating whales (in winter) or a playful school of dolphins (all year) in the ocean.

If there is surfing action at The Wedge, admire the daring athletes, otherwise enjoy the view from Jetty View Park towards Corona State Beach and the boats passing the harbor channel. You can even venture out to the tip of the jetty (watch your steps). Return the same way to Balboa Pier. If you are tired, use the paved walkway from F Street on, if you still feel fresh, continue along the shore, since the view of the glistening ocean is so splendid, and you do not want to miss the chance of observing sea life. After arriving at Balboa Pier enjoy a snack or a healthy lunch. Return the same way.

Modification: If you want more exercise, start and finish at Newport Pier.

Jogging/Running: You have a choice of the boardwalk or the sand.

Running at the beach

Beach fun near Newport Pier

Trip: From Newport Pier to Balboa Pier (Round Trip) or to West Jetty (Round Trip) Running

Rating: ●●●●◖
Distance: From two to six miles.
Difficulty: Easy
Best Time: All year at low tide.
The Run: For the jogger it is fine to follow the same path as the walkers do. For the serious runner it is not so much fun on the boardwalk, since the pavement is not good for the knees. Therefore, we prefer to start at Newport Pier and run along the beach, since its flat here, and the sand is tightly packed, which makes it a good surface to run on.

However, that changes after Balboa Pier. From now on up to The Wedge you have two choices, either continue on the edge of the water where the conditions can be very tough (uneven surface, surf coming up), or run in the sand further back from the water, where the sand is very deep, to challenge your muscles.

Modification: If you do not want that much exercise, make Balboa Pier your turning point.

Inline Skating: The Boardwalk at Balboa Peninsula is well paved and flat, so it's great fun gliding along, even though you have to share it with all other outdoor enthusiasts, and the speed limit is just eight mph.

Bikers crowd the boardwalk on weekends

Trip: F Street to 36th Street (Round Trip) Inline Skating, Biking

Rating: ●●●●◖
Distance: Six and a half miles roundtrip.
Difficulty: Easy
Best Time: All year, crowded on summer days and weekends.
The Trip: After having parked the car near F Street, glide along Ocean Front Boardwalk and enjoy the picturesque architecture to your right and the endless sandy beach and the ocean to your left. Staying on Ocean Front you pass Balboa Pier, watch out at the parking lot for the traffic, then glide on passing Newport Pier and continue to 36th Street.

Return the same way. Stop at Balboa Pier for your snack, since near F Street there are no eateries.
Biking: It is scenic going along the boardwalk, but for cyclists slower traffic can be disturbing, especially on weekends and during holidays.

Trip: From 36th street to the Wedge (Round Trip) Biking

Rating: ●●●●
Distance: Twelve miles, about an hour.
Difficulty: Easy
Best Time: All year, weekday mornings.
The Ride: Follow the boardwalk passing Newport Pier and Balboa Pier up to F Street, where it ends. Turn left and continue south on Balboa Boulevard, which down here is no longer crowded. Follow it until it ends at West Jetty Park. It is fun watching the vessels in the harbor mouth. Return the same way.

Las Arenas Sports Park on Balboa Peninsula

Basketball court on Balboa Peninsula

Sailboat passing the harbor channel

■ Formal Sports Activities
Tennis, Volleyball, Basketball,
Other Ball Games

Usually, you don't find too many opportunities at the beach for more formal activities, but at the Peninsula this is different. The sports facilities of the elementary school between 13th and 14th Street are right by the beach and include a grassy field for use after school hours. Also, the peninsula is at some places so narrow that a facility located on the other side of Balboa Boulevard might be only steps from the beach.

Tennis: Between 16th and 17th Street four public tennis courts (free) in Las Arenas Park, which even have backboards on the courts.
Volleyball: Several nets near Balboa Pier, also one net near Newport Pier.
Basketball: Four full courts on the school premises, not in very good shape, but with great surroundings; half court at Las Arenas Park
Other Ball Games: Grassy areas at the school grounds and at Balboa Park.
Combo: Combine any actiity with a good swim in the Pacific. You feel refreshed and your muscles will loosen up.

Harbor view from Balboa Peninsula

Newport Beach Harbor

→ Bayside Drive County Beach
→ China Cove Beach
→ Rocky Point Beach
→ Balboa Island

Rating: ●●●●◖

Best Time: All year, especially during weekday mornings.

Location: Newport Beach Harbor is protected from the ocean by the "finger" of Balboa Peninsula.This outer harbor is four miles long and runs parallel to the coastline and Pacific Coast Highway. It is contained within Newport Bay and is referred to as Lower Newport Bay.

Access: There are many choices to access the outer harbor. All access routes start off Pacific Coast Highway, which divides Newport Bay.

Profile: Newport Harbor, one of the finest small boat harbors in the world has an open water area of about 6000 acres, and is giving shelter to about 10.000 boats.

Touring the harbor by boat and observing its seven man made islands is a true feast for the eyes. You can even meet marine mammals like dolphins or seals during your trip, as well as many seabirds.

The beach front areas surrounding the harbor offer opportunities for walking, running, bicycling, swimming, as well as for volleyball or mere sunbathing.

Balboa Island, one of those seven man made harbor islands is unique, since you can encircle it on foot enjoying harbor and yacht views..

Bayside Drive County Beach, China Cove Beach, Rocky Point Beach

Rating: ●●●●◖, for swimming ●●●

Best Time: Spring and fall, very crowded in summer.

Access: Access is on Bayside Drive or further south on Ocean Boulevard. From PCH take Marine Avenue down to the water. Before the bridge to Balboa Island turn left into Bayside Drive, which after roughly a mile becomes Ocean Boulevard. Limited street parking.

Profile: The are the most prominent calm beaches and boat launching opportunities (Bayside Drive Beach) on the inland side of Newport Harbor.

Facilities: Restrooms at Bayside Drive County Beach. At Rocky Point Beach use the facilities of adjacent Big Corona Beach. See p. 66.

Carrying a kayak at Bayside Drive Beach

Bayside Drive County Beach is right next to the Orange County Harbor Department at 1401 Bayside Drive It is the largest of the inland beaches facing the harbor. Here it is easy to launch a kayak.

There is also a volleyball net.

China Cove Beach is a small sandy cove close to the harbor channel, is located off Ocean Boulevard at Farnleaf Street. Pedestrian access is from Shell and Cove Streets, stairs at Ocean Boulevard between Fernleaf and Dahlia Avenues.

Rocky Point Beach (Pirates Cove) is a scenic little beach framed by rocks off Ocean Boulevard at the southwest side of the harbor mouth next to Big Corona Beach.

It is not the best place for swimming, but it is a great place as a stopover on your kayak tour through the harbor and for watching the boats passing the harbor channel. Also, to watch sunsets from the top of the rocks that frame it is a delight.

Movies were shot here, and it is a very much sought after setting for wedding pictures. Access is by stairs or over some rocks from Big Corona Beach.

Beach fun at Pirates Cove

Stand up paddeling in Newport Beach

Kayak trip in Newport Beach Harbor

Canoeing in the harbor channel

■ Water Activities
Swimming, Canoeing, Kayaking, Rowing

Swimming: Calm beaches have their pros and cons. The advantage especially for small children and less skilled swimmers is that those beaches are well sheltered from the ocean, there is no surf. On the other hand calm beaches in harbor areas are usually more polluted than the open waters.

Canoeing, Kayaking and Rowing: If you really want to get to know the harbor, going by boat is almost a must.

SUP (Stand Up Paddeling): It is becoming more and more popular in Orange County, mostly in harbors, but expert dare big waves also.

Sailing: Within the frame of this guide we cannot go into details about sailing, but if you stay longer in the area, you should definitely check this great – though somewhat costly sport. Instruction in NB is offered at:

Orange Coast College Sailing Center, 1807 West Coast Highway.

Newport Sea Base, 1931 West Coast Highway.

Trip: Balboa Island Loop
Kayaking, Canoeing

Rating: ●●●●◖

Difficulty: Easy, but you need some physical fitness, if you want to go the full distance.

Distance: 2.5 miles (up to an hour, depending upon your ability), 4.5 miles for the modification (up to two hours).

The Trip: You can choose your starting point. If you bring your own boat, Bayside Drive County Beach is a good choice for easy launching. If you rent a boat, the closest place is right at the ferry landing on Balboa peninsula.

The route is simple, you cannot miss it. However, be very careful with the traffic if you have to cross the main channel of the harbor at the beginning and at the end of your trip. We suggest circling the island clockwise. You can stop at one of the tiny calm beaches on North

Rock climbing at Rocky Point Beach

Bay Front of Balboa Island facing inland.
Modification: If you are in good physical condition, you can extend your trip, if you circle Harbor Island and Linda Island in addition.

Go in the direction of Pacific Coast Highway bridge. Right before the bridge you must turn right. You will first pass under Aloha Drive Bridge. If you then keep to your left you will pass under Harbor Drive Bridge. At the end of Harbor Island you must turn right to arrive back at your Balboa Island loop starting point.

■ Other Activities

Rock Climbing: At Rocky Point Beach you can combine beach activities with some rock climbing.

Little Balboa Island viewed from Balboa Island

Balboa Island
Rating: ●●●●◐

Access: You turn off Pacific Coast Highway at the intersection of Jamboree Road and Marine Avenue. Take Marine Avenue down towards the ocean; after the traffic light cross the bridge and you are right there. Parking on Balboa Island is possible either on Marine Avenue, which is usually crowded, or in any of the smaller side streets (free).

Profile: Balboa Island is a charming little man made island, which is interesting to the active person, since you can walk or jog around it, while enoying spectacular views of different parts of the harbor.

In part of Balboa Island, you can still admire the cute beach cottages, which were so common in the 20th century in the Newport Beach area.

Facilities: None on Balboa Island.

For the Hungry and Thirsty: Park Avenue Café at the corner of Park Avenue and Agate Street. You can sit outdoors. Concession stands at the ferry landing. Also many restaurants line Marine Avenue.

■ Trail Activities
Walking, Jogging

The paved walkway around Balboa Island is the only one that lets you enjoy the outer harbor on foot. You can either walk or jog (sorry, no bicycles or inline skates).

Trip: Around Balboa Island
Walking

Rating: ●●●●◐

Distance: A little over two and a half miles.

Difficulty: Easy

The Trip: The starting point depends upon your parking place.

If you are parked near Marine Ave, you start

Harbor and Balboa Pavilion from the walkway around Balboa Island

Walking around Balboa Island

walking or jogging down North Bay Front counterclockwise. Walk two thirds of a mile and end at the tip of the island where a small bridge leads to Collins Island (which is private). On the other side of the island you can watch the ferries and other boat traffic passing forth and back. You will also recognize Newport Landing, the historic landmark of Newport Beach.

Enjoy the busy harbor life on your way down to the other end, which you cannot reach directly, since a channel divides the island. Walk or jog north (inland) along the channel and admire some of the old small beach cottages, leftovers of a time past. Then cross the bridge at Park Avenue and circle this separate part of the island called Little Balboa Island until you are back at the bridge. Walk or jog inland on Marine Avenue, where you have the choice of many small eateries.

Modification: You can park your car near Park Avenue and Agate (that is the street, where the

Big Corona Beach from Ocean Boulevard

small ferry takes off) and start your walk or jog from where the ferry lands.

This way you will finish near Park Avenue Café at the corner of Park Avenue and Agate.

Corona del Mar State Beach (Big Corona Beach)

Rating: ●●●●◖, for scuba diving ●●●●
Best Time: Any
Location: A few blocks from Pacific Coast Highway at Ocean Boulevard and Iris Avenue
Access: In the community of Corona del Mar turn west from Pacific Coast Highway toward the ocean onto Marguerite. Drive to the end of the road, turn right onto Ocean Boulevard. Park in the street (free) or drive down after fifty yards on your left hand side to beach parking lot (fee). From Ocean Boulevard walk down the car ramp, or turn southeast and walk down the stairs at Narcissus Avenue.

Profile: Big Corona Beach as locals call it is located at the south eastern side of the harbor channel opposite the famous Wedge on Balboa peninsula. It is sheltered by rocky cliffs, on top of which expensive houses overlook the beach. This one half mile long stretch of fine sand and gentle surf is Newport's preferred family beach. Crowded in summer, and on holidays.

Facilities: Wheelchair access, fire pits, showers, restrooms, drinking water, life guards.

Other Attractions: Boats passing the harbor channel, sunsets over Catalina Island; watch from the rocks or from Lookout Point.

Enjoy a fire in the evening at one of the fire pits. Come early; they are very much sought after.

Also, seals, pelicans, and other marine life species can be observed at times.

For the Hungry and Thirsty: Snacks at the concession stand and the restaurant at the beach parking lot. Very popular vegetarian Zinc Café is a few blocks away on 3347 East Coast Highway.

■ Water Activities
Swimming, Scuba Diving, Snorkeling

Swimming: This sandy beach is good for swimming, especially for children. The surf stays mostly moderate.
The water usually gets an A-rating (check the regional papers for ratings).
Scuba Diving: Inspiration Point at the southeast end of the beach is a good area with easy access. It is one of our favorite dives, since the water is most often clear and marine life is plentiful close to the reefs.
Your entry point is next to the big rock jutting out of the ocean near the beach.
Swim out towards the buoys. About forty feet southeast from the southern most buoy protecting the safe swim area lies the first of two different reefs with abundant marine life to enjoy. This one has a big overhang for the diver to swim under and mingle with the garibaldi (California's state fish). A bit further out the reef rises to a steep hill giving access to fish in tiny caves and holes.
Southeast from this reef lies another reef peaking up from the ocean bottom to about

Snorkeling at Little Corona Beach

thirty feet high providing ample environment for reef fish. Also small gorgonian, starfish and other species can be found on the reefs.
On our swim back over the sandy area we once spotted some halibut and a leopard shark.
Snorkeling: The rocky area at the southeast end of the beach (Inspiration Point) is a great snorkeling spot.
Less experienced snorkelers should venture out only if the surf is low.

■ Trail Activities
Jogging

A run just on Corona del Mar State Beach is too short to give you good exercise. But you can have fun jogging, and improve your conditioning, if you start at the jetty and jog to the other end of the beach, then jog up the stairs,

A surfing lesson for the dog

Big Corona Beach

Cliffs at Little Corona Beach in the evening sun

run back on Ocean Avenue on top of the cliffs, jog down the car ramp and continue to the jetty. Repeat according to your fitness.

■ Formal Sports Activities
Volleyball: Eight nets

Little Corona Beach

Rating: ●●●●◖
Best Time: Late spring, summer and fall. The beach is crowded in summer and on holidays.
Location: Newport Beach, Community of Corona del Mar, near Big Corona Beach.
Access: In Corona del Mar turn west from Pacific Coast Highway toward the Ocean onto Marguerite. Drive to end of the road, turn left onto Ocean Boulevard. Drive to the end of the street and look for a parking place in the street (free). The paved ramp down to the beach is rather steep.
Profile: This great small beach is mostly known

to locals. It is great for people looking for a quiet spot. Little Corona Beach is very close to Big Corona Beach. At low tide you can walk from one to the other. It is easily identified by its arch rock, on it south eastern end, which makes a nice object for pictures.
It is also a great place for snorkeling.
Facilities: Restrooms, showers half way up the ramp. Life guards (seasonal).
For the Hungry and Thirsty: Bring a picnic.

■ Water Activities
Swimming, Snorkeling, Scuba Diving, Yoga

Swimming: The waters here mostly are calm, which makes it a good beach for children. Water quality is often Grade A. Check local papers for daily ratings.
Snorkeling: Pretty good at the northwest end of the beach near the rocky area (see image above).
Scuba Diving: Little Corona Beach is well

Migrating birds at Upper Back Bay

suited for beginning and intermediate scuba divers at the rocky reefs.

Yoga: A private yoga group meets Wednesday mornings. Feel free to join!

Combo: You can combine swimming with snorkeling or yoga or make it your starting or ending point for a beach hike to or from Crystal Cove State Park at minus tide (see p. 85).

Upper Back Bay

→ North Star Beach
→ Newport Dunes Waterfront Resort and Marina
→ Back Bay Trails

Rating: ●●●●●
Best Time: All year; best for bird watching: November
Location: Between Pacific Coast Highway and Jamboree Road in Newport Beach
Access: You can choose from several access points and parking areas.

If you come from Freeway 405 or Toll Road 73, take Jamboree Road exit, going toward the Pacific. Jamboree Road crosses the northern end of Back Bay. You can park on either side of Back Bay, either take a right turn before the bridge into Bayview Way and park (free), or turn right after the bridge into East Bluff Drive and park there (free).

If you come from Pacific Coast Highway, take Jamboree Road inland and turn left at the first traffic light into Back Bay Drive. Park in the street just before Back Bay Drive hits the Bay, or proceed slowly (15mph) to the parking lot right at the Bay after about a mile plus (free).

Profile: Upper Back Bay reaches from the harbor bridge (PCH) up to Jamboree Road. Almost 900 acres of it belong to the Upper Newport Bay Nature Preserve on the north and north-west side of the bay and the Upper Back Bay Ecological Reserve.

The Ecological Reserve is an estuary, where about 200 species of water birds live; it is also

Rowing practice, Back Bay

a stopover for migrating birds on the Pacific Flyway, and a winter resort for some of them.

Back Bay Loop is a twelve plus mile path around upper Back Bay and through the Nature Preserve, where hikers, joggers, bikers, horse back riders, and inline skaters share the trails. They can admire the scenery of water, cliffs, and mountains, and watch the many birds.

Horseback riding is restricted to areas on the north and northwest side.

On the waters of Back Bay you can canoe, kayak, and row. North Star Beach with the Newport Aquatic Center, and Newport Dunes Resort, a private enterprise are the two gateways to water activities.

Special Features: The Back Bay Science Center is located at Shellmaker Island on 600 Shelmaker Road off Back Bay Drive north of the Dunes. It is open to the public for special events only. Canoe tours and walking tours start from Shellmaker Island.

Free "Friends" walking tours start from the lookout point on the corner of Back Bay Drive and Eastbluff at the northeast end of Back Bay Drive every other Saturday.

The Muth Interpretive Center on 2301 University Drive at the corner of University and Irvine Avenue offers exhibitions and interactive displays about the Estuary.

For the Hungry and Thirsty: Dock at Back Bay Bistro at the entrance to Newport Dunes Aquatic Park across the Bay from NAC and enjoy their famous Clam Chowder. Or enter their parking lot from Back Bay Drive.

For people finishing their activity near Jamboree Road, there are eateries at the corner of Bristol Street and Jamboree, one plus block inland.

For people finishing at the Aquatic Center Haute Cakes at 1807 Westcliff Drive is a litttle bit off your route, if you are on foot or are biking, but it takes just a few minutes if you drive. The food is healthy and tasty.

Back Bay in winter

Newport Aquatic Center

outrigger canoeing, besides being a training center for national and international teams.

NAC offers a choice of water environment: You can either enjoy paddling or rowing through the calm waters of beautiful Back Bay, or use the direct access to Newport Harbor and the ocean. The NAC offers hourly rentals; you can also get a monthly membership, that entitles you to use all the equipment including, the kayaks, canoes, and rowing shells (after the member has been certified by an NAC employee).

If you live in Orange County, you can get a yearly (family) membership. If you own a boat, there is limited storage space at NAC.

■ Water Activities
Kayaking, Canoeing, Rowing, Swimming

Swimming: One is permitted to swim at North Star Beach, and it is a calm water beach, but here the grayish sand looks rather uninviting and the water does not look great either.

Trip 1: Back Bay - Upper Newport Bay
Kayaking, Canoeing

Rating: ●●●●●
Best Time: All year, also great at full moon.
Distance: Up to 5.8 miles.
Difficulty: Easy, but some conditioning is required.

North Star Beach
Rating: ●●●●● Boating, ●●◐ swimming
Best Time: All year.
Location: One Whitecliffs Drive.
Access: From PCH go to Dover Drive, turn right on Westcliff Drive, right on Santiago Drive, right again on Polaris Drive and right on Whitecliffs Drive. To your left are North Star Beach and Newport Aquatic Center (NAC).
If you come from Freeway 55 exit at 17th street, take a left on Dover Drive, turn immediately right on Westcliff Drive, right at the stop sign on Santiago Drive, right again on Polaris Drive, and right on Whitetcliffs Drive. On your left you will find North Star Beach and the NAC. Parking is free.
Profile: The beach here is sandy, and you got a great view of Back Bay and its white cliffs rising above both shores. If you are looking for an activity in human powered crafts in Orange County, the Newport Aquatic Center (NAC) is the place to start.
This non-profit corporation is located directly on the shore of Upper Back Bay in Newport Beach. Within its 18000 square foot facility it offers the public unique opportunities in water sports like rowing, canoeing, kayaking and

Kayaking close to white pelicans

Profile: The calm waters of Newport Bay also permit the less experienced kayaker or canoer to safely enjoy the activity on the water.

If you are not that athletic, it is wise to check the tide charts before you start, to make sure you go up the Bay when the water comes in and go towards the ocean, when the water goes out.

The roundtrip to the end of Upper Newport Bay at Jamboree is one of the top kayak or canoe trails nationally, and takes about one and a half to three hours, depending on your paddling skills and the tides.

Facilities: Showers and restrooms at the NAC for members.

Special Features: One of the few trips in California, where you can observe the life of an estuary first hand.

Combo: One of our favorite activities is combining a bicycle ride around Back Bay (compare p. 74) with one of the boating trips. If you can spare more time (about four hours), then it is fascinating to begin with a trip atop the bluffs, and then conclude as an 'insider'. It is a worthwhile experience.

The Trip: Launch your boat at North Star Beach. Paddle towards the hills and make sure you follow the main channel, since it is not permitted to use the side channels; most of them dead end anyway.

Depending upon the policies, you can go all the way to Jamboree Road, or you have to stop at a sign midway, which says: "From here on birds only". You will not only enjoy the chalky cliffs of Dover Heights, but also observe the birds of the Bay as an insider.

Trip 2: Back Bay– Newport Harbor - Balboa Island
Kayaking, Canoeing

Rating: ●●●●◖
Best Time: Weekdays
Distance: Up to seven miles.
Difficulty: easy, some conditioning required.
Profile: Newport Harbor with its views of seven picturesque residential islands, its numerous mansions, and more than 9000 boats is a feast for the eyes and is lots of fun to be discovered by self-guided tours.

If you are not a paddling expert, make sure you stay out of the way of big boats. For safety reasons, explore the less crowded parts of the harbor on the inland side of Lido Island, Linda Island, Harbor Island and Balboa Island first, until you can handle the harbor traffic. You can choose your boating time. If you are an expert, and paddle the harbor all over, you can spend well up to two hours.

The Trip: As an intermediate paddler, launch your boat at NAC and go towards the harbor. Paddle under the PCH bridge and turn left immediately. You paddle along Linda Island and pass under Aloha Drive. Keep to your left and pass under Harbor Island Drive and go along Harbor Island.

At the end of Harbor Island you will have to make a sharp right turn and face Balboa Island. Circle Balboa Island clockwise. Then continue straight; you have Harbor Island to your right. Turn right and leave Lido Island to your right. Continue paddling to Pacific Coast Highway where you pass under the bridge and return to the Aquatic Center.

Newport Dunes Waterfront Resort

The calm beach at the Dunes with bridge

Newport Dunes Waterfront Resort

Rating: ●●●●（, swimming ●●●（
Best Time: Late spring and early fall, when the crowds are gone.
Location: Near Pacific Coast Highway, at Back Bay Drive close to the corner of Jamboree Road.
Access: If you come from PCH, turn inland at Jamboree Road. Turn left at the first traffic light into Back Bay Drive, and then another left into the Dunes parking lot (fee). If you come from 405 take Jamboree Road exit, go towards the Ocean; turn right at Back Bay Drive.
Come by bike or walk to avoid a fee.
Profile: Newport Dunes Waterfront Resort is a private enterprise, open to the public. Among other amenities, it features a picturesque, secluded beach with fine white sand which stretches for a mile. It is sheltered from the ocean breezes, with a great view of Back Bay.
Facilities: Restrooms.
Special Features: The Dunes Resort has cottages for reasonable rent as well as an RV Park with a freshwater swimming pool and spa.
For the Hungry and Thirsty: There is a small store, The Market Place, at the Dunes, where you can get drinks and a snack, or you can walk to the Back Bay Bistro, which sits a little further north across the parking lot right next to the public launching dock.

■ Water Activities
Boating, Swimming, Windsurfing, Sailing

Boating: The Dunes are a very good location for launching your canoe or kayak. You can also rent one on site. For trip suggestions see p. 71.
Swimming: The sandy half moon shape beach at the Dunes is a calm water beach. Even though

Back Bay Drive

the water looks clean, we cannot recommend it for swimming, since the vicinity of boat traffic in the neighborhood can pollute the water.
Windsurfing and Sailing: Lessons offered.

■ Trail Activities
Walking, Jogging, Biking

Walking, Jogging: It is a nice and easy twenty minute walk, or an even shorter jog on the water's edge around the lagoon, crossing the water on the small bridge that links the shores. Of course, you can also start your Back Bay loop bike ride from the Dunes (see the following pages).

■ Formal Sports Activities
Volleyball: Volleyball net at the beach.

Back Bay Trails
Rating: ●●●●●
Best Time: Any
Distance: Up to ten miles.

Difficulty: Easy to moderate.
Profile: It is great to circle Back Bay on trails. The roundtrip is called Back Bay Loop and was recently marked right on the paved trails. We will inform you which part of the trail system is best fotr the activity of your choice.
For the Hungry and Thirsty: See p. 70.

■ Trail Activities
Biking, Jogging, Walking, Inline Skating, Horseback Riding

Profile: It is great to circle Back Bay on trails. The plus ten miles round trip is called Back Bay Loop and was recently marked right on the paved trails. We will describe the loop and inform you, which trails of the area are the best for the activities of your choice.

Trip: Back Bay Loop
Biking

Rating: ●●●●●
Best Time: All Year.
Distance: Ten plus miles (about an hour plus).
Difficulty: Easy, with the exception of two short rather steep inclines.
The Ride: Biking around the bay is a great experience and the best way of doing the loop. Of course, you can start anywhere.
To us it seems the best way to start at the north

Biking on Back Bay Drivel

View of PCH bridge and the harbor from Upper Back Bay

end of Back Bay. Park your car either on the eastern or western side of the Bridge, on Bayview Way or Eastbluff Drive respectively. You can go clockwise or counterclockwise.

If you do the trip counterclockwise, you will find an eating place at about two thirds of your trip, and you will have to master this steep little hill at the end. You can once more admire Back Bay from the lookout point on top.

Follow the bikeway towards the ocean. (If you park on Eastbluff Drive, you have to cross the bridge on Jamboree first). You share it with horse back riders, joggers, hikers, and - where paved – with inline skaters. Cross a wooden bridge and ascend a couple of hundred feet.

Veer to the left after passing the Interpretive Center on your left, following the bikeway that parallels Irvine Avenue. Be careful, where it descends steeply.

At the corner of Irvine Avenue and Santiago Drive turn left into Santiago Drive. You ride through quiet neighborhood streets after turning left on Galaxy Drive.

Stop at Galaxy Park on your left, a small park with a fascinating view of Back Bay and its bluffs.

Follow Galaxy Drive a bit further, then turn left at Polaris Drive, which goes downhill, and again left on Whitecliffs Drive for a scenic short detour to North Star Beach and the Newport Aquatic Center, and enjoy Back Bay and the Bluffs from the Bay level. (Our route here is

Egret walking Back Bay

Inline skating at Back Bay in Newport Beach

slightly different from the marked loop where you do not go down Polaris Drive).

Return to Polaris Drive, which goes further downhill, before it goes uphill quite a bit after a curve to the right. At the top turn left into the bikeway that will parallel the Bay up to Castaway Park for an easy but most scenic ride. Castaway Park is the very best lookout point on your trip. You will see the harbor, the ocean, Catalina Island at times, Fashion Island, and Back Bay with its Bluffs. In spring part of the park is covered with a carpet of flowers.

Descend on the bike path that parallels Dover Street. Be careful here, it is very steep and it will lead right to Dover Street, which you follow a bit before you turn left on Pacific Coast Highway. Cross the bridge, which separates the harbor from Back Bay and turn left into the first street, which is Bayside Drive.

You have entered Newport Dunes Resort. Follow the road to a wooden pedestrian bridge to cross the Bay. (See image p. 73).

After the bridge keep to the right on your way through the parking lot to the closest exit to Back Bay Drive, where you turn left.

Back Bay Drive is open to one-way automobile traffic (15mph), and is one of the busiest exercise routes in Newport Beach. You will share the street with others on feet or on wheels. If you love watching birds, this is the section of Back Bay Loop to do it.

At the end of Back Bay Drive you ascend a short but steep incline. On top of the hill stop at the lookout point and give Back Bay a final glance.

Then ride down Eastbluff Drive to your parking spot or continue further and cross the bridge on Jamboree Road, in order to return to Bayview Drive.

Walking, Hiking: In case you want to walk all of Back Bay Loop, you are out for a day's hike (XXL). If you just want to walk one to two hours, we suggest either the Back Bay Drive part of the loop, starting in either direction, or the Upper Newport Bay Ecological Reserve area on the opposite side of the Bay. There you find numerous trails to choose from; you cannot get lost.

Jogging: Jogging around Back Bay is an exercise of an hour and a half or more. For shorter jogs we recommend the same areas as for walking.

Horseback Riding: The area for horseback riding is the Upper Newport Bay Nature Preserve, on the western shore of Back Bay.

Horseback riding at Back Bay

The track at Corona del Mar High School

Newport Beach City Parks and Recreational Facilities

▩ Formal Sports Activities

Tennis, Baseball/Softball, Basketball, Soccer, Lawn Bowling, Track and Field, Lap Swimming

The over forty city parks and recreational facilities of Newport Beach other than beach parks are very well kept. The majority of them provide facilities for more formal sports activities.

Besides, there are several public golf courses in Newport Beach.

Also, the school sport facilities including the outdoor swimming pool in Newport Beach are open to the public, if not used by the schools.

In this guide we introduce just a few of those that are either attractive, because of their opportunities for exercising, and/or because of their great location, and design.

Bonita Canyon Sports Park
Rating: ●●●●

Location: Bonita Canyon Drive and Mesa View Drive in Newport Beach

Access: From PCH take McArthur Boulevard, turn right into Bonita Canyon, right into Buffalo, then right for tennis, basketball and soccer, left for baseball, softball. There is a parking lot, street parking is also possible.

Profile: This is the largest of Newport Beach's sports parks. It covers two unconnected areas, which are about a quarter of a mile apart. It is very well maintained.

Bonita Canyon Sports Park

Tennis at Bonita Canyon Sports Park

The tennis courts are used frequently, since they dry easily and they are located in an area protected from wind.
Facilities: Drinking fountain, barbecues, picnic tables, two large play areas, restrooms.

Tennis: Two tennis courts in excellent shape.
Baseball/Softball: Four youth baseball/multi-purpose fields.
Basketball: One full basketball court.
Soccer: One soccer field.

Irvine Terrace Park
Rating: ●●●●●
Location: Seadrift Drive at Evita Drive.
Access: From PCH turn seawards at Irvine Cove turn left into Seadrift Drive. Parking on the street (free).

Profile: Among the many community parks of Newport Beach this park is outstanding.
This multi-purpose sport park is not crowded, and since its location is somewhat hidden, it feels very private.
You cannot only play a game of basketball or a game of tennis, but also walk or jog on a path that circles the soccer fields. Since this path is paved it makes an excellent course for skateboarding or inline skating.
In addition, there are benches in a nicely landscaped area, from where you can enjoy a grand view of the harbor and the Pacific.
Facilities: Barbecues, picnic tables, great play area, water fountain, restrooms.

Basketball: One full court.
Inline Skating, Walking, Jogging, Inline Skating: A paved path that circles the soccer fields.
Soccer: Two smaller soccer fields.
Tennis: Two tennis courts which are also used for classes by the Recreation Department.

San Joaquin Hills Park
Rating: ●●●●
Location: San Joaquin Hills Road and Crown Drive.
Access: From PCH take Jamboree Road, turn right into Joaquin Hills Road and again right into Crown Drive. There is a parking lot.
Profile: This is a small park, and mentioned

Irvine Terrace Park

Lawn Bowling Club at San Joaquin Hills Park

here especially since it houses the Newport Beach Lawn Bowling Club, where membership and even instruction are free.

Facilities: Water fountains, restrooms at the Bowling Club.

Lawn Bowling: Active Lawn Bowling Club.
Tennis: Four tennis courts, no lights. At certain hours these courts are used by the Newport Beach Recreation Department for instruction. They are also very popular among seniors.

Corona del Mar High School
Rating: ●●●●
Location: 2120 Eastbluff Drive, Newport Beach.
Access: From PCH. Take Jamboree Road to Eastbluff Drive.

Profile: We have selected the Corona del Mar High School sports facilities in this guide, since the Marian Bergeson Aquatic center is open to the public to lap swimming for a nominal fee, mostly on weekends and weekday mornings.

Also, track and field athletes enjoy morning and evening exercises, when students are not present.

Besides, Newport Beach's residents can play a game of tennis on the four tennis courts open to the public (free), when school is not in session, and teams do not practice.

Facilities: Restrooms in the pool area.

Swimming: A nice competition size pool.
Tennis: Eight courts, four courts open to public.
Track and Field: Artificial surface track.

Newport Beach Golf Course
Rating: ●●●◖
Location: 3100 Irvine Avenue Newport Beach.
Access: From PCH go to Jamboree, turn left on Bristol and left on Irvine Avenue.
Profile: Actually this golf course is not the nicest place on earth, since it is too close to Orange County Airport and your concentration is constantly tested by jets roaring above your head.

But on the pro side one has to mention it is the least expensive course in the area.

18 holes, driving range.

Facilities: Restaurant, snack bar, restrooms.

Pool at Corona del Mar High School

Newport Beach Golf Course

Beach life near Historic District at Crystal Cove State Beach

General Area Crystal Cove State Park

→ **Crystal Cove State Beach**
→ **Crystal Cove State Park**

www.crystalcovestatepark.com

Orientation:

The rolling surf of the Pacific Ocean, the wide, sandy shoreline and the close to ninety feet high bluffs, which represent the first of several former marine terraces, characterize the coastal portion of Crystal Cove State Park.

The gently sloping hills, the high ridges above Moro Canyon of the 2400 acres undeveloped wilderness inland provide hikers, joggers, bikers and horseback riders with eighteen miles of trails and stunning views of the back country, the coastline, and the islands out in the Pacific Ocean as well.

The park is not only one of Orange County's largest areas of natural seashore and wild open space in the backcountry, it is also a true piece of paradise left between housing, resort and shopping developments along the coast. The adjacent Laguna Coast Wilderness Park permits you to extend your activity adventures into Laguna Beach. (See Laguna Beach p. 93)

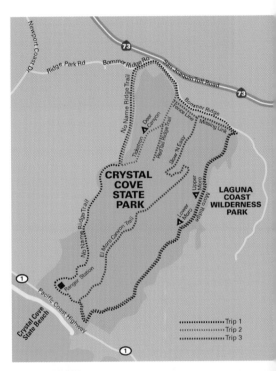

Crystal Cove State Beach

Rating: ●●●●●

Best Time: All year. In spring the colors of wildflowers and the fresh greens of various plants on the cliffs add an extra flavor.

Location/Access: Right on Pacific Coast Highway.

From Pacific Coast Highway between Newport Beach and Laguna Beach there are five entrance points – three of which are for cars.

Pelican Point: This is the first entrance for cars

Spring at Crystal Cove State Park

Sunset viewed from Crystal Cove Beach

coming from Newport Beach. For cars you pay a fee; bikers and hikers are free. This northernmost entrance to the park has four bluff top parking areas. Trails that take a couple of minutes lead to rather steep access ramps. If you follow the path that parallels the bluffs in direction of Pelican Hill Golf Course, you can also descend a stairway to the beach and the tide pools on this end of Crystal Cove Beach.

 If you don't mind an extra walk along PCH and then along a paved path through the bluff tops, you can park for free in the neighboring streets west of PCH and enter via the pedestrian path right at the beginning of Crystal Cove State Park.

Los Trancos: The Los Trancos parking area is the largest parking lot. It is located on the inland side of PCH, south of Pelican Point entrance. It is the furthest away from the water. In addition to the street crossing at the traffic light a pedestrian underpass leads to the beach and the historic cottages. There is also wheelchair access.

Reef Point: This entrance for cars is the closest to Laguna Beach. There are two parking lots very near the beach. A stairway descends down to the beach, as does a steep paved ramp (Muddy Creek Ramp) to the south.

From El Moro Canyon Trail in Crystal Cove State Park on the western side of PCH there is a tunnel to the beach at El Moro Cove, a little south of Reef Point that can be used by hikers. However, the tunnel is to be shared with the waters that come down the hills, and therefore can at times be passed barefoot only, due to high tides or rain water streaming down from the foothills.

Facilities: Portable toilets at end of some access ramps. Showers, restrooms, drinking fountain, picnic tables on bluff tops next to parking lots.

Profile: This more than three miles stretch of natural seashore offers seven separated coves with wide sandy beaches bordered by cliffs, covered with dense shrubs, colorful in spring. Trails with spectacular views meander through the coastal bluff tops.

The area is miraculously detached from the busy world represented by nearby PCH.

Come on weekdays – in spring and early summer after morning fogs have cleared – and you will have this marvelous place all to yourself, whether you are out for swimming, surfing, snorkeling, tide pool exploring or just walking or sunbathing.

Even during holidays and vacation times you will find an empty stretch of beach, if you are willing to stroll through the sand for a couple of hundred feet before you settle down.

Special Features: The 1140 acre Underwater Park, which has been created within the

Pelican Point access ramp, Crystal Cove

Ochre Sea Star - a tide pool treasure

The so called Historic District, consisiting of over forty cottages, dating back to the late twenties and early thirties of the previous century is another attraction at Crystal Cove. Many cottages were recently renovated or even rebuilt to maintain the historic character. About two thirds of them are open as vacation rentals. **For The Hungry And Thirsty:** At Shake-Shack, a seventy-five year old smoothie-stand that also serves sandwiches, on PCH at the southern part of the park, you get a great view, while enjoying your food. If you drive south on PCH you cannot miss the little white hut.

The Beachcomber, a restaurant in the Historic District in a unique location right at the beach; it is very convenient, but crowded and pricy.

boundaries of Crystal Cove State Beach extends 120 feet offshore and protexts the marine wildlife. It is not permitted to take any samples The underwater park makes a great playground for scuba divers and snorkelers.

The many tide pools, especially at north western end of Treasure Cove, at Pelican Point, and at Reef Point area exhibit abundant sea-life.

Other Attractions: Enjoy spectacular views of Catalina Island, especially when the sun sets behind it in winter.

Watch whales from December to February as well as other sea-life, best from the bluff tops at the very northern end of the park above Treasure Cove.

■ Water Activities

Swimming, Body Surfing, Surfing, Snorkeling, Scuba Diving, Boating

Swimming: Due to rocky reefs submerged in the water at higher tides, you have to be careful with swimming at certain places. Since after storms the sand is often shifted, the rock free areas can change quite a bit. Ask the life guards, where one can swim safely. We found the safest place at all seasons and under all conditions southeast of the Reef Point area.

At the Historic District Area swimming is best

Boogie boarding at Reef Point, Crystal Cove

Scuba divers at Crystal Cove Beach

Surfing in the evening sun

just southeast of the Los Trancos creek mouth, just northwest of the rocks. Also, the area just southeast to the point where the most northern ramp from Pelican Point entrance hits the beach at Treasure Cove, is mostly rock free.

It is relatively safe for small children, to play or bathe in or near the water at Crystal Cove State Beach, since it is mostly shallow, where the

Snowy egret walking at Crystal Cove Beach

water meets the sand. However, be very careful at times, when surf is high.

Water quality usually gets an A rating here. It can change after storms. Consult the regional paper: The Orange County Register.

Body Surfing, Boogie Boarding: El Moro Beach close to Reef Point is liked best by boogie boarders.

Surfing: Treasure Cove near the access stairs, Reef Point and south part of El Moro are best.

Scuba Diving: The best areas are at Reef Point and at Pelican Point at the south eastern end of Treasure Cove; experts are attracted to the Corsair F4U crash site further out at Reef Point.

Snorkeling: Crystal Cove Underwater Park is a good area even for not too experienced snorkelers, especially good southeast of Historic District, and near Muddy Creek Ramp, where historic anchors are placed. If you are not an expert, ask the park staff to advise you, where it is best to enter.

Active at Reef Point, Crystal Cove Beach

Boating: Of course you can launch your kayak or the like anywhere at Crystal Cove Beach, but if you do not want to carry your boat too far, it might be best at Historic District, since there is car access close to the beach.

■ Trail Activities
Walking, Hiking, Running, (Biking)

Since the sand is well packed at Crystal Cove State Beach, the ocean front is very well suited for running, hiking or walking. You can start and finish wherever you like, the round trip is 6.4 miles. Tailor it according to your ability.
You also may hike, run, or bike a variety of bluff top to beach loops on paved paths.

Trip 1: Treasure Cove to Abalone Point - (Round Trip)
Running (Hiking)

Rating: ●●●●●
Best Time: At low tide.
Difficulty: Easy
Distance: (Roundtrip) almost six miles.
Profile of the Run (Hike): At high tide there might be some small rocks to overcome, the shore is even, the sand firm.
The Run (Hike): Descend the stairs or the ramp to Treasure Cove. Then follow the shore line. Close to the ocean the sand is very firm.

Modification: On your way back get up the ramp at Reef Point and move along a path on the bluff top. Enjoy the view of hills on one side and of the ocean and islands on the other side.

Trip 2: Treasure Point to Little Corona Beach (Round Trip)
Hiking

Rating: ●●●●◖
Best Time: Minus tides. (Consult a tide table).
Difficulty: Moderate. (There are a few rocky areas, some might require a little bit of rock climbing. Protect your feet).
Distance: Roundtrip: 2.5 miles .
Facilities: Restrooms, showers, drinking fountains and picnic tables on bluff tops near the parking areas at Crystal Cove; restrooms, showers, drinking fountain halfway up the ramp at little Corona Beach.
Profile of the Hike: This short distance walk requires more time than you might expect, since it turns into rock hopping part of the way. Stop on the way and admire some of Orange County's richest tide pool areas. At minus tides rocky

Exploring rocks on a beach hike

Mussels exposed at low tide, Crystal Cove

the architectural beauty of a mansion that sits there on top of the cliffs. Admire or photograph the rock formations near the shore. If you are careful you can even climb them.

Since the grounds are mostly covered with small rocks or pebbles you cannot walk too fast anyhow. After you have passed about six more coves that involve some easy rock climbing you will see Arch Rock, to which you might be able to walk to at very low tide. This is also the sign that you have reached Little Corona Beach. Return the same way, possibly after a swimming break.

Modification: If you are in company of other drivers and you just want a shorter workout, drop a car at Little Corona Beach at the corner of Ocean Boulevard and Poppy Avenue, and finish your hike there, take a good swim, enjoy the tide pools, and then pick up the other car at Crystal Cove State Beach.

Combo: What makes Crystal Cove State Park so unique besides its natural beauty is the opportunity to enjoy so many different activities. Combining them is almost a must here. For instance, to cool off after a jog or hike along Crystal Cove State Beach (pp xxx) or after a mountain bike tour or a hike in Crystal Cove State Park on the inland side of Pacific Coast Highway (pp. xxx) by swimming in the Pacific afterwards is great fun.

reefs are exposed to a degree that let you study abundant marine life.

The Hike: Descend the stairway down to Treasure Cove. Enjoy the tide pools at the northern end of the rock framed beach. Step carefully over the rocks and walk along the shoreline of the small cove.

While you continue walking or are resting on a sandy spot at the next cove, you might admire

A Marbled Godwit among a flock of ploves

Moro Canyon, Crystal Cove State Park

Crystal Cove State Park

Rating: ●●●●●

Best Time: Dry season, since park closes after rainfall. Cool season, morning or late afternoon hours in summer.

Location/Access: 8471 Pacific Coast Highway Laguna Beach.

There are two entrance points:

1. Main Entrance: Turn inland off PCH about two and a half miles south of Newport Beach (Sign El Moro Canyon) and drive up to the Ranger station. Plenty of parking spaces are available (fee).

2. Bommer Ridge Road Entrance: From 73 toll road exit Newport Coast Drive and go south towards the ocean. Turn left on Ridge Park Drive. Take Ridge Park Drive all the way up until it dead ends. Parking is free.

Facilities: Restrooms, drinking water at Park Headquarters, main entrance.

Special Features: Three nice wilderness campgrounds, one in the valley, two at higher elevations, no facilities.

For the Hungry and Thirsty: Upper Moro Ridge Campground, Lower Moro Ridge and Deer Canyon Campground invite you for a rest and a picnic, if you bring supplies.

After you leave the park (main entrance), turn right on PCH and then right again into Crystal Cove Shopping Center. Find Whey Café for refreshments which you can enjoy outdoors.

On your way back (Bommer Ridge Road entrance) cross Coast Newport Drive and stop at Sharky's Mexican Grill in the Newport Coast Shopping Center for a snack.

A Gartersnake at Crystal Cove State Park

Hiking through the mustard fields, Crystal Cove State Park

■ Trail Activities
Hiking, Running, Mountain Biking,
Horseback Riding

Trip 1: Ridges and Park Boundaries
Mountain Biking, Hiking

Rating: ●●●●◖
Distance: Ten miles (700 feet elevation gain).
Difficulty: Getting up to Bommer Ridge Road –
intermediate, going back on Moro Ridge Trail –
easy. The short ride down on B.F. I. Trail –
difficult.
The Trip: This is our favorite trip in the park,
whether it is on bike or on foot.
From the main parking lot go northeast towards
No Name Ridge Trail. Follow the trail which
climbs up to the ridge. The views up here are
spectacular. Ride along No Name Ridge Trail,
which has some steep inclines. Avoid all the
trails to your right; they go into the canyon.
Shortly after you pass the Ticketron turn off, you
actually leave the park boundaries. Towards the
new developments along Ridge Park, the trail
turns into a well groomed horseback riding and
jogging trail. Follow it until you come to a fork.
Turn right and bike back into the wilderness.
You are on Bommer Ridge Road now which is
part of the Laguna Wilderness Park, paralleling
the Crystal Cove Park boundaries.
At post sign Bommer 5 re-enter Crystal Cove
Park at gate 12 on Moro Ridge Trail. This part of
your trip towards the Pacific Ocean offers the
most spectacular views over the wilderness and
Moro Canyon.
Turn right on B.F.I Trail and carefully descend.
If you are not an expert, demount and walk down
this short trail.
At the bottom turn left and soon right to take a
left, when it joins El Moro Canyon Trail and
then a right which brings you to the fire road
behind the school and back to the parking lot at
the Ranger Station.
Modification: (XXL). We often do this trip as a
day hike. It is great, but it takes much more than

The fun of running ....

.... and biking in Crystal Cove State Park

the two hours we usually take for exercising
(five plus hours). Take water, since this is dry
country.
Combo: Take a swim in the ocean after the trip
is refreshing ands will relax your muscles.

Trip 2: Deer Canyon Round Trip
Hiking, Jogging

Rating: ●●●●◖
Distance: 3.5 miles (700 feet elevation gain).
Difficulty: Moderate
Best Time: Cool season, or early morning
hours.
Profile: This area with great vistas is popular
late afternoon, and in the early evening with
mountain bikers, runners and hikers, who come
here exercising after work.

Sandstone cave in Moro Canyon, Crystal Cove State Park

The Hike/Run: You start out after parking at the end of Ridge Park Drive. Turn right and follow the wide trail (which is first a community trail and then part of Laguna Canyon Wilderness Park) about one mile to Crystal Cove Park entrance gate Nr. 22, where No Name Ridge Trail starts.

Keep walking or running a bit further until Ticketron starts at your left. Follow it (it turns into Deer Canyon Trail) to Deer Canyon Campground nestled under ancient trees. The picnic tables at the campground invite you to a short rest and maybe a snack. Continue up the hills to Red Tail Ridge Trail, and turn left there. Continue up to Bommer Ridge Road, where you enter Laguna Coast Wilderness Park. Turn left and walk or run back on Bommer Ridge Road to your entry point.

Trip 3: Moro Canyon – Moro Ridge Roundtrip
Mountain Biking, Running, Hiking

Rating: ●●●●◖
Distance: Seven miles (700 feet elevation gain).
Difficulty: Easy (in the valley and on the ridge).

moderate (going up and coming down). The single track along the fence line is difficult for mountain bikers.

Best Time: Cool season, early morning, late afternoon, since the trails are exposed to sun.

Profile: During the first half of your trip you are on the most popular trail in Crystal Cove Park. After you climb up to the ridge you will enjoy the views this park is famous for.

The Trip: You start at the Ranger Station going towards PCH. Above El Moro Elementary School turn left. Stay on this fire road until El Moro Canyon trail, where you turn left. Diverse native plants line the path which mostly parallels the Moro Watershed. Part of the year the creek to your right might carry water.

A Prickling Pear cactus beginning to bloom

The sandstone cave off to your right is just one off many rock formations in the park. Also realize, that this canyon was populated already thousand of years ago by Native Americans.

Don't miss Slow N Easy Trail turning off to your left. It takes you up slowly to a ridge. On the top turn right into Fence Line Trail. Make sure you do not go down Elevator Trail to the right. It is very steep and takes you right back into the canyon.

Instead take a short left and then a right again onto Fence Line/ Missing Link, which is a single track and somewhat tricky to maneuver. Follow it until you reach Moro Ridge Trail. Turn right onto Moro Ridge Trail and proceed as in Trip 1 via B.F.I. Trail, and then after the junction with El Moro Canyon Trail bike, run or hike back to the parking lot the same way you came. Take water!

Moro Ridge trail near Pacific Ocean

Modification: Since this trip takes longer for runners and hikers than the time we usually exercise, you can shorten it by turning right onto I Think I Can Trail (East Cut Across Road) after about one mile into the canyon.

It takes you up to El Moro Ridge Trail quite steeply. The elevation gain is close to 700 feet. At the junction with El Moro Ridge Trail turn right and proceed as above. This roundtrip is four miles.

California Poppies

The tower at Victoria Beach in South Laguna

General Area Laguna Beach

→ **North Laguna Beach**
→ **Central Laguna Beach**
→ **South Laguna Beach**
→ **Laguna Beach City Parks and Other Sports Facilities**
→ **Laguna Coast Wilderness Park**
→ **Aliso and Wood Canyons Wilderness Park**
→ **Laguna Niguel Regional Park**

www.lagunabeachinfo.org
www.ocparks.com
www.lagunaniguel.com
www.beachcalifornia.com/laguna-beach-beaches

Orientation:

Laguna Beach including South Laguna Beach is Orange County´s city with the most beaches. Most of the thirty public beaches are tiny cove and pocket beaches along a seven mile stretch of steep cliffs. So, if you are looking for privacy, here you can find it here. However, if you want to socialize on the beach, the two large beaches Main Beach Park and Aliso Creek County Beach will guarantee you a young and lively crowd almost all year long.

In Laguna many of Pacific Coast Highway´s side streets towards the ocean end either in a view point on top of the towering cliffs or lead to a steep stairway, which descends to yet another sandy cove, where the sand might completely disappear at high tide.

Laguna, the artist city among the beach cities, has one great disadvantage though. There is just room for one highway between the top of the ocean bordering cliffs and the steep hills inland.

Cliffs at Laguna Beach

Hiking in Laguna Coast Wilderness Park

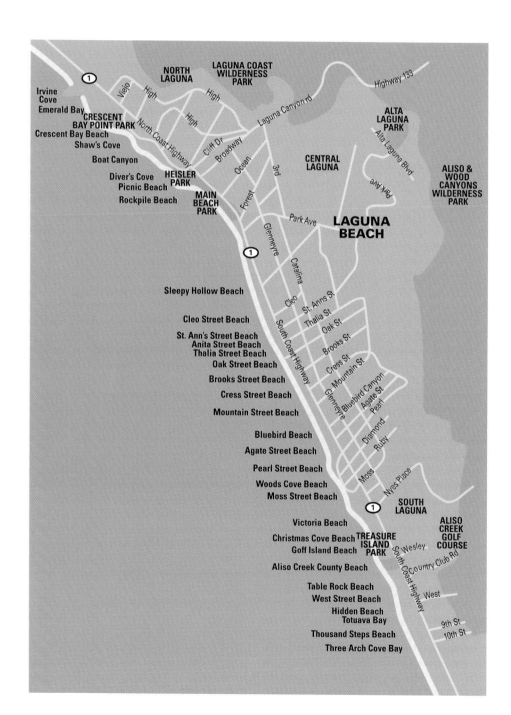

Beach life in North Laguna Beach

That makes parking at most of the small beaches very difficult and often leads to a traffic jam along PCH. The good news is, that almost all of the beaches can be accessed by the OCTA bus.

We will list all of the beaches here, yet we will concentrate on those, that are outstanding.

We also divide Laguna in three areas – north, central and south.

Laguna Beach is a true paradise for active people, loving water activities: Swimming and all kinds of surfing, diving and snorkeling are a must here, since Laguna has plenty of rocky outcroppings, which host many species.

Options for trail activities are also numerous: Beach hikes or beach runs in Laguna Beach will give you great exercise and stunning views at the same time.

In addition to magnificent beaches Laguna Beach boasts an amazing wilderness area of 6.600 acres.

Laguna Coast Wilderness Park, on the inland side of PCH in North Laguna, is a recent addition to the many parks in Orange County. It is open to hikers, runners, mountain bikers, and horsemen.

You have the choice of many trails, where views of the coast line or Laguna Beach are common. Besides, the park connects to Crystal Cove State Park (p. 87), and to Aliso Wood and Canyons Wilderness Park.

Aliso Wood and Canyons Wilderness Park stretches from the hilly inland side of Laguna Beach to Laguna Niguel. Its trails lead through beautiful and diverse nature; they are frequented by hikers and by expert mountain bikers.

Laguna Niguel Regional Park is a small marvel close to the inland border of Aliso Wood and Canyons Wilderness Park.

More formal sports are offered at Main Beach Park or at beautiful Alta Laguna Park among others.

Emerald Bay, North Laguna Beach

North Laguna Beach

Rating: ●●●●◖

Best Time: Any time weekdays.

Profile: North Laguna Beach covers the area from the northern border up to Main Street. Several picturesque coves draw visitors and locals to the beach sheltered by towering bluffs. Heisler Park which lines the bluffs is magnificently landscaped and provides for nice walks with amazing views.

For the Hungry and Thirsty: The many picnic tables seem the first choice for a snack.

Mexican restaurant Las Brisas near Heisler Park towards the southern end of Cliff Drive overlooks Main Beach and the ocean. You can eat outdoors or have a drink at the outdoor bar. Young people prefer this restaurant during the day. It is often crowded, making metered parking spaces in the street hard to get.

On the inland side of PCH there is a small restaurant called Madison Square and Garden Cafe, where you can have breakfast or lunch outside and even bring your dog.

■ Water Activities

Swimming, Scuba Diving, Surfing, Boogie Boarding, Skimboarding, Snorkeling, Boating

Irvine Cove and Emerald Bay

Swimming, Boating

Rating: ●●●●

Best Time: Late spring, summer, and fall.

Profile: Both of these wonderful beaches in the very north of Laguna with fine white sands are framed by rocks. There is no landside public access yet, so you have to come by kayak or canoe. They are nice for a picnic and a swimming break, if you are ocean kayaking.

Crescent Bay Point Park and Beach

Swimming, Scuba Diving, Surfing, Body Surfing, Boogie Boarding, Snorkeling

Rating: ●●●●

Best Time: All year, for swimming best late spring, summer (weekdays), and fall.

Location: The most northern public beach of Laguna is part of Crescent Bay Point Park at Crescent Bay Drive.

Access: Access to the bluff top park is easy. From PCH you turn towards the ocean at Crescent Bay Drive, which takes you right to the park on top of the bluffs. . Parking is free either at Crescent Bay Drive or at adjacent Cliff Drive.

Either take the stairway from Circle Drive down to North Crescent Bay or go down the short steep paved ramp from Cliff Drive to the southern part of the beach.

Profile: The beach is a sandy six hundred yards

Seal Rocks from Crescent Bay Park

Shaw's Cove in North Laguna

cove with rocky areas at the north and south end. It is one of the bigger and more scenic beaches. Expect it to be crowded on weekends and holidays.

The bluff park on top offers 180-degree vistas of the ocean and Laguna Beach.

Seal Rocks, on the northwest side of Crescent Bay, is host to seals and sea lions; this area is also great fun for scuba divers, who have to swim out about a hundred yards.

The beach is level where it meets the water, but surf is strong at times, up to fifteen feet. Watch out, if you come swimming accompanied by children. Water quality is mostly graded as an A.

Facilities: Restrooms, showers, water fountains, lifeguards (seasonal).

Special Features: At the north end of the cove you will find a major tide pool area.

Other Attractions: The Laguna Art Museum above the north Laguna Beaches on 307 Cliff Drive at the intersection of PCH.

Shaw`s Cove
Swimming, Scuba, Diving, Boogie Boarding, Snorkeling, Boating

Rating: ●●●● (Beware of occasional strong surf and rock bottoms on the south side).

Best Time: Late spring, fall and weekdays in summer.

Location/Access: On the end off Fairview Avenue off PCH. Limited metered parking is on

Boat Canyon at high tide

A summer day at Picnic Beach in North Laguna Beach

Fairview Avenue. Access by ramp and stairway.
Profile: Shaw's Cove is about 500 feet long.
Swimming, boogy boarding, scuba diving (also
for beginners) and snorkeling are good or very
good here. It is one of the most popular diving
spots in Laguna. Also, it is a good beach to
launch a boat.

Most often this beach is well protected from big
waves, and currents. Water quality is usually A.
Facilities: None

Boat Canyon (Fisherman's Cove)
Scuba Diving, Boating
Rating: ●●●, for underwater activities
●●●●
Best Time: Late Spring, summer, and fall.
Location/Access: It is just south of Shaw's
Cove. Take Wave Street off PCH to Cliff Drive.
From the 800 block on Cliff Drive a steep dirt
path leads down to the water. A narrow paved

trail also leads down to Boat Canyon just before
the staircase that takes you to Diver's Cove, the
next beach.
Profile: This tiny hidden sandy beach is great
for scuba diving due to the rocky ocean floor.
Boat launching is very convenient. Sand can
disappear at higher tides.
Facilities: None

Diver's Cove:
Scuba Diving (easy), Swimming (shore
breaks, watch out), Body Surfing.
Rating: ●●●◑
Best Time: Late spring, summer (weekday
mornings for parking) and fall.
Location/Access: Diver's Cove joins Picnic
Beach at its southern end. You reach it via a
narrow stairwa off Cliff Drive. next to the path
to Boat Canyon (Fisherman's Cove). Turn off
Pacific Coast Highway at Myrtle or any other

street in North Laguna to Cliff Drive and park at the few metered parking spots in the 600 block off Cliff Drive.

Profile: Swimming, scuba diving (easy entry), and body surfing are popular at this three hundred feet long sandy family beach. Diver's Cove is within the Underwater Park Ecological Preserve. Therefore, don't take any samples.

Facilities: None, but excellent facilities on the next beach (Picnic Beach).

Picnic Beach
Swimming, Surfing, Scuba Diving, Snorkeling
Rating: ●●●●, for swimming ●●●◖
Best Time: Late spring, summer (weekday mornings), and fall.
Location/Access: Off PCH at Myrtle Street to Cliff Drive, just below Heisler Park. Metered parking on Cliff Drive. Walk through Heisler Park and descend a paved ramp to the beach.
Profile: This protected cove below Heisler's Park is one of the larger beaches in North Laguna – about seven hundred feet long. It is a

The gazebo in Heisler Park

popular family beach, which can get crowded during weekends and holidays. Watch out for rocks in the center when swimming.

Picnic Beach is another beautiful spot for diving and snorkeling. Turn to the left of the ramp. There are several smaller reefs, that snorkelers and divers like to explore.

Other Attractions: Beautiful landscaped Heisler Park on top of the cliffs is a delight for walking the one plus mile, overlooking the ocean and Laguna, or having a picnic.

Facilities: Showers, restrooms, life guards (seasonal), picnic tables in Heisler Park.

Rockpile Beach (Rocky Beach)
Scuba Diving (rather for advanced divers), Surfing, (no swimming or body boarding).
Rating: ●●●◖
Best Time: All Year.
Access: Turn off Jasmine Street off PCH to Cliff Drive (metered parking). You can take the stairs down to the beach either at the northern or the southern end of the cove.
Profile: This small rocky cove below the southern end of Heisler Park stretches about seven hundred feet and is the least crowded of the diving spots in North Laguna.

At high tide, the sand might disappear, at low tide you can almost walk to Birds Rock, a bird sanctuary close by in the Pacific; keep a safe distance though, since people are not permitted.
Special Features: Tide pools.

Rockpile Beach in North Laguna Beach

Main Beach in Central Laguna from Heisler Park

■ Trail Activities
Walking, Jogging

It is a must to walk or jog the coastline in North Laguna, whether it is on top of the bluffs or down at the beach.

Rating: ●●●●◖
Best Time: Weekdays all year. Very crowded on weekends and holidays.
Trip: Crescent Bay Park to Heisler Park (to Laguna Main Beach to Woods Cove).
Rating: ●●●●◖
Best Time: All year weekdays.
Difficulty: Easy to moderate.
Distance: One and a half miles, three miles, or six miles depending on your route.
The Walk/Jog: After you have enjoyed the view from Crescent Bay Park, walk or jog down the stairway, directly off Circle Drive, walk or jog along Crescent Bay Beach, up the ramp on the southern part of the beach to Circle Drive,

continue on the boardwalk for a few blocks until you enter Heisler Park. Stroll or run through the beautifully landscaped park above Diver's Cove, Picnic Beach and Rock Pile Beach.
Take the extra turn to the gazebo at the southern end of Heisler Park, where you can observe the action at Birds Rock. After that follow the stairs down to the wooden boardwalk at Main Beach. Continue a little further to the end of Main Beach. Make it a one way and stay at the beach, or return the same way.
Modification 1: If you want less exercise, stay on top of the bluffs until you pass the gazebo. Then follow the trail down to Main Beach.
Modification 2: If you want more exercise, you can extend your trip all the way to Woods Cove. For this hike or run low tide is optional as the sand can disappear at the smaller beaches during high tide. Some of the rocky cove linings, which at low tide require minor or no climbing, would otherwise become serious obstacle. Iff you are surprised by rising water,

don't try your luck. Instead walk or run up the access stairs, hike along thel street to the next beach, and descend the stairway to continue along the water. Such a trip along multiple beaches gives you a good workout and is fun.

Central Laguna Beach

Rating: ●●●●◐

Profile: The coast of Central Laguna has its greatest attractions at Main Beach, where you find a gap in the cliffs. Further south it gets more and more scenic; numerous pocket beaches are hidden below towering cliffs.

In summer and during holidays the major Central Laguna beaches are very crowded, since Laguna Beach attracts many tourists.

To top it off, Main Beach is a favorite for expert basketball and volleyball players.

■ Water Activities

Swimming, Scuba Diving, Snorkeling, Body Surfing, Boating

Main Beach

Swimming, Scuba Diving, Snorkeling

Rating: ●●●●◐

Best Time: All year weekdays. Extremely crowded during weekends and holidays.

Location/Access: At heart of town right where Pacific Coast Highway meets Broadway and Ocean Avenue.

Examining the catch

Access is easy; you cannot miss it, if you drive on Pacific Coast Highway, but parking is a problem, as there are few metered parking spaces on PCH or in nearby streets.

Profile: Main Beach is the place to go for those who want to see and be seen. This about half a mile long beach is also the center of physical activity in Laguna Beach year round. It is often very crowded, since everything is so close.

A nice sandy beach with no hidden rocks in the water, invites you to swim and sunbath. The surf is rather low most of the time. Therefore Main Beach is good for family swimming.

Diving and snorkeling is at its north end, where access is also from Rockpile Beach.

You can launch a hand carried boat from Main Beach; but parking near the beach is close to impossible, which makes boat launching difficult.

Surfing is not allowed during summer months.

Facilities: Restrooms, showers, drinking fountains, picnic tables, life guards (seasonal).

For the Hungry and Thirsty: Picnic tables at Main Beach Park; many eateries across Pacific Coast Highway.

Sleepy Hollow Beach

Swimming, Surfing,Body Boarding

Rating: ●●●◐, ●●●● for swimming

Best Time: Late spring, summer and fall.

Location: It is the next beach south of Main Beach on Sleepy Hollow Lane, off Pacific Coast Highway in Central Laguna.

Access: A stairway on Sleepy Hollow Lane leads you down to this small sandy beach, which is mostly used by guests of a hotel, which sits on the bluffs above this beach. You can also reach this beach by walking south from Main Beach, since it is adjacent to it.

Profile: This beach is good for swimming. There are no hidden rocks in the water and the surf breaks evenly here. If you are looking for a less crowded place with calm conditions close to downtown Laguna, this is the beach to go to.

Facilities: none

Cleo Street Beach/St.Ann's Street Beach

Scuba Diving, Surfing, Body Boarding,

Rating: ●●●● for diving, ●●●◖ for surfing.

Location/Access: Off PCH on Cleo Street/St. Ann's Street. Limited meter parking on Cleo Street/St. Ann's Street. Stairways lead down to these small pocket beaches, or you can walk from Main Beach.

Profile: Small, but scenic coves. The old wreckage about two hundred yards offshore at Cleo Street Beach attracts divers. Rocky bottoms are hazardous for swimmers. Beaches can disappear at high tide.

Facilities: None

Thalia Street Beach

Surfing, Skimboarding

Rating: ●●●●

Best Time: All Year.

Location/Access: At Central Laguna Beach, off Pacific Coast Highway at Thalia Street, limited meter parking. Access is by stairs.

Profile: This scenic beach is a surfing beach and not good for swimming, because of rocky reef bottoms. There are good reef breaks.

Facilities: None

Surfer enjoying the ride

Sun bathing at Thalia Street Beach

Anita Street Beach

Swimming, Surfing

Rating: ●●●◖

Best Time: Late spring, summer, and fall.

Location/Access: Off Pacific Coast Highway at Anita Street in Central Laguna. Stairs lead down. Limited metered parking on Anita Street.

Profile: Another small, sandy beach that is connected to Thalia Street Beach and Oak Street Beach. Most of the season you will find locals on this beach.

Facilities: None

Oak Street Beach

Body Boarding, Body Surfing, Swimming (at the northern end)

Rating: ●●●◖

Best Time: Late spring, summer, and fall.

Location/Access: Oak Street, off PCH. Access is by stairway. Limited Parking on Oak Street.

Profile: Small sandy beach that is connected to Anita Street Beach. It is similar to the beaches north and south of it.

Facilities: None

Brooks Street Beach

Surfing

Rating: ●●●●◖

Location/Access: Off PCH at Brooks Street. A stairway gets you to the beach. Limited meter parking on Brooks Street.

Profile: This is a top surf spot in Laguna, where surfing is best with a good south swell. The Brooks Street Summer Surf Classic takes place at this beach.

Facilities: None

Cress Street Beach

Scuba Diving (experienced divers only), Surfing

Rating: ●●●● for scuba diving and scenery, ●●● for other activities.

Best Time: Any time (for scuba divers the surf should be moderate.

Location/Access: Off PCH at Cress Street in Central Laguna's shopping, hotel and restaurant district. It sits below a rather steep stairway. Limited meter parking on Cress Street.

Profile: This very scenic sandy beach is marked by a big rock. It is sought after by scuba divers. It cannot be recommended to swimmers and body surfers, since the shore breaks can be very dangerous to the head and neck. Rip currents.

Facilities: Lifeguards (seasonal).

Active at at Oak Street Beach

Mountain Road Beach

Scuba Diving, Body Surfing, Swimming

Rating: ●●●◖

Location/Access: It follows Cress Street Beach to the north and connects to Bluebird Beach to the south. A stairway goes down to the beach. Limited parking on Mountain Road.

Profile: A wide sandy stretch below a large hotel. However, some submerged rocks, reefs, and rip currents make this a tricky beach.

Facilities: None

Cress Street Beach

Bluebird Beach

Swimming (not at southern end), Body Surfing, Body Boarding

Rating: ●●●◖

Location/Access: At the corner of South Coast Highway and Bluebird Canyon a ramp leads down to the beach. Limited parking on South Coast Highway.

Profile: It is a sandy beach below a large hotel, with some small reefs at the southern end.Hotel guests and locals frequent this beach. Body boarders and body surfers handle the strong shore breaks. Watch out when swimming.

Facilities: None

Agate Street Beach

Surfing (in summer limited), Swimming

Rating: ●●●◖

Location/Access: Runs along Agate Street off PCH. Limited meter parking; stairs.

Profile: A small sandy beach with rocks and an arch rock at its southern end that connects it to Pearl Street Beach.

Facilities: None

■ Trail Activities

Walking, Jogging

Trip: Main Beach to Woods Cove (roundtrip)

Walking, Jogging

Rating: ●●●●

Best Time: All year weekdays, extremely crowded on weekends and holidays.

Distance: Between one and five miles roundtrip.

Difficulty: Easy, no elevation gains, firm sand.

The Trip: Start on Main Beach and walk or jog along the beach to Sleepy Hollow Beach and continue to Woods Cove.

■ Formal Sports Activities

Basketball, Volleyball

Main Beach

Basketball: Even though there are only two half courts available, this is a place for very skilled basketball players during weekends and holidays. It is fun to watch.

Walking along Cenral Laguna Beaches

Volleyball at Main Beach Park

Basketball at Main Beach Park

Volleyball: The three beach volleyball courts attract experts on weekends and holidays.
Combo: Laguna Main Beach offers itself to a combination of activities..

South Laguna Beach

■ Water Activities

Swimming, Surfing, Scuba Diving, Body Boarding, Skimboarding, Snorkeling

Pearl Street Beach
Body Boarding, Scuba Diving, (no surfing)
Rating: ●●●◐
Location/Access: Off Pacific Coast Highway at Pearl Street. Limited meter parking. Access the beach by stairway.
Profile: Small cove framed by rocky reefs. Locals enjoy this private little beach.
Special Features: This is one of the six top tide pool areas in Laguna Beach.
Facilities: None

Woods Cove Beach
Surfing, Scuba Diving, Swimming (watch out)
Rating: ●●●●, for swimming ●●●◐
Best Time: Late spring, summer and fall.
Location/Access: Easy access off Pacific Coast Highway from Diamond Street. Limited metered parking on Diamond Street or Ocean Way. A stairway framed by beautiful plants and flowers leads down to the beach. There is another access just to the north off Ocean Way.
Profile: Nice sandy cove framed by rocks. Locals and visitors alike enjoy the privacy of this beach and its sea sculptured rocks.
Special Features: Tide pools.
Facilities: None

Moss Cove Beach
Scuba Diving, Snorkeling, Swimming
Rating: ●●●
Location/Access: Off Pacific Coast Highway on Moss Street.

The beach is accessed by stairway. Limited meter parking on Moss Street or Ocean Way. Profile: Moss Cove Beach sits south of Wood's Cove It is tiny and sheltered by steep cliffs. Small and large rocks (the southerly rocks are called Moss Point) are scattered around the beach; the sand disappears at high tide. At this less crowded beach you will mostly find nearby living locals and divers.

Special Features: Great tide pools (low tide).
Facilities: None

Victoria Beach
Swimming, Scuba Diving
Rating: ●●●●◖
Best Time: Late Spring, summer, and fall.
Location/Access: You access Victoria Beach by taking Victoria Street off Pacific Coast Highway. Walkway and stairs lead you down to the water. Parking on Victoria Street is almost impossible. Park on PCH.
Profile: Victoria Beach is another great beach in Laguna. The locals like it for its soft white sand and its blue green water. If you are out for solitude, this is your beach at least on week days. The water is good for swimming and often gets an A rating.
Other Attractions: There is a tower built in 1926, which was designed to provide spiraling stairs from the cliffs above; it looks like a medieval construction and makes a great object for photos at the northern end of the beach.

For the Hungry and Thirsty: In the shopping center off PCH on Montage Resort Drive, you will find two restaurants and also a coffee shop.

Treasure Island Park and Beach
Christmas Cove, Goff Island
Scuba Diving; (Goff Cove Beach):
Swimming, Snorkeling, Kayaking
Rating: ●●●●●, for swimming ●●●●
Best Time: Late Spring, summer, and fall.
Location: At Wesley Street and Pacific Coast Highway in South Laguna. This beach is located at the ocean side of Montage Resort and Spa.
Access: You have to use the very parking on Pacific Coast Highway and walk down some stairs and through the park to the two ramp (wheelchair accessible) to the ocean.
Since the bus stop is very close to the entrance of Montage Resort and Spa we strongly recommend leaving your car at home. Or park at the next beach to the south: Aliso Creek County Beach (fee) and walk north.
Profile: This great park is Laguna's most recent addition to its numerous beach parks. It is not an island; the name comes from the movie Traesure Cove, which was shot here.
This park on top of the bluffs stretches from the highway to the beach and is beautifully landscaped.
The area covers Goff Cove Beach with Goff Island and Christmas Cove. It is connected to Victoria Beach and to Aliso Creek Beach. This

Woods Cove

Victoria Beach

Treasure Island Park and the beautiful sandy coves below, Laguna Beach

park and beach is one of our favorites.
The surf is not too high, but there are some rocky areas. It breaks at the shore. Goff Cove Beach, however, is protected from high surf. The water is mostly clean.

Facilities: Restrooms, outdoor showers on top of the bluffs, drinking fountains, picnic tables, lifeguards (seasonal).

Special Features: Tide pool areas.

For the Hungry and Thirsty: The shopping center across PCH has a Chinese restaurant, which is open for lunch. There is also a coffee shop.

Aliso Creek County Beach
Swimming, Surfing, Skim Boarding, Diving (recommended for experienced divers), Boating
Rating: ●●●●
Best Time: Late spring, summer and fall.

Location/Access: Easy, since it is right at Pacific Coast Highway in South Laguna. The large parking lot with metered parking is next to the sand, almost at the water. You can also park on the far side of PCH, where an underpass leads to the beach. Wheel chair access is from Treasure Island Park.

Profile: This beach became very popular, when South Laguna was developed. In summer it is crowded with young people and families. The beach is wide and sandy, and covers a little less than a mile of shoreline. Water and sand often meet at a steep angle. This place is a skimboarder's delight. Scuba divers like it, as it is not too crowded.

The surf at times is rather high, the waves breaking with a crash onto the sand, which makes it difficult for inexperienced swimmers and children.

But we also went swimming here, when surf

Aliso Creek County Beach from Treasure Island Park

was low, and swimming seemed good for everyone. The smallest surf seems to be at the northern end of the beach.

Water: Due to Aliso Creek emptying into the Pacific here, water quality at times is not very good. Check the local papers!

Facilities: Restrooms, showers, lifeguard (seasonal), picnic tables, fire pits, playground.

Special Features: Tide pools at the rocky promontories.

For the Hungry and Thirsty: There is no concessionaire here since the pier was torn down, but there might be one in the future.

Table Rock Beach
Swimming (be careful, rocks)
Rating: ●●●
Best Time: Low tide.
Location/Access: Off Pacific Coast Highway at Table Rock Drive. Limited meter parking. A rather new stairway leads down to the Pacific Ocean.

Profile: This small, about four hundred feet long beach with rocks is mostly known to locals. Sand can disappear at high tide.

Facilities: None

West Street Beach
Swimming, Surfing
Rating: ●●●●
Best Time: Any time.
Location/Access: Off Pacific Coast Highway at West Street in South Laguna. There are two staircases descending down to the beach. Limited metered parking at West Street.

Profile: This very nice beach has an extensive sandy shore. The surf is often low, which is good for swimming; surfing is best at the south end near the rocks.

Facilities: Pit toilets, seasonal lifeguards.

▣ Formal Sports Activities
Volleyball

Volleyball: Two volleyball nets at this beach.

Totuava Bay, Hidden Beach
Swimming, Boogie Boarding
Rating: ●●●●(

Location/Access: Presently, there is no landside access to these beautiful neighboring beaches. Either you climb over rocks coming from 1000 Steps Beach (see below), or you have to access it via canoe or kayak.

Profile: Totuava Bay is a scenic sandy cove. Hidden Beach is a tiny sandy cove adjacent to Totuava Bay, framed by large rocky bluffs.

Totuava Bay, Laguna Beach

1000 Steps Beach
Swimming, Surfing, Diving
Rating: Over all ●●●●, for diving ●●●●(

Best Time: Late spring, summer and fall.

Location: In South Laguna between 9th and 10th streets off Pacific Coast Highway

Access: Limited parking on Pacific Coast Highway (metered).

Even though there are only about 220 steps down to the beach (it just feels like 1000 steps), running up or walking up fast can be a challenge, and a good conditioning exercise.

Profile: This is another tucked away beautiful medium size sandy beach, framed by rocks. It is a locals' favorite. Surf is often high, so it better suits advanced swimmers. It is also a Marine Preserve; therefore you cannot take anything away. The water is clean.

Facilities: Showers, restrooms, lifeguards (seasonal).

West Street Beach, South Laguna Beach

Skimboarding at Hidden Beach

Three Arch Cove Beach
Swimming, Surfing
Rating: ●●●
Location: Beach in South Laguna south of 1000 Steps Beach with no landside public access.
Profile: Small rocky beach, where sand might disappear at high tide. Well known and liked by the home owners on top of the bluffs for its very scenic three arch rocks.

■ Trail Activities
Walking, Hiking

Trip 1: Victoria Beach to Aliso Creek County Beach (Roundtrip)
Walking
Rating: ●●●●◖
Distance: 2.5 miles.
Difficulty: Mostly easy.
Best Time: Low tide.

Access: See Victoria Beach p. 106.
Profile: Beach hiking is not easy at most South Laguna Beaches, since many of the pocket beaches are framed by rocks. The hike starting at Victoria Beach goes all the way to Aliso Creek Beach.
The Trip: On Victoria Beach turn south and do not mind some minor rock climbing on the way. Pass Treasure Island, Goff Island and then hike all the way to Aliso Creek County Beach. Walk along this larger beach, and return the same way. The round trip can take up to two hours. In summer cool off in the ocean on your way.

Trip 2:: Valido Trail and West Street
Beach Hiking, Jogging
Rating: ●●●◖
Distance: Two miles.
Difficulty: Moderate
Best Time: Dry season because trail is closed after rainfall.
Access: From Pacific Coast Highway in South

Bluff area plant in spring

Laguna after Aliso Beach turn inland on West Street, left on Valido Drive. Trailhead is ahead on left hand side.
The Trip: Hike up Valido Trail which is quite steep until you reach Aliso Summit Trail where you turn left. Ascend further to the summit of Aliso Peak. This is another short but steep climb.
At several view points you will be rewarded with spectacular ocean views and stunning vistas into Aliso and Wood Canyons Wilderness Park. After you reach the summit turn around and head back down the same way.
Combo: You can combine the trail hike with a beach hike and a swim at West Beach.
Directions: See West Street Beach p. 108.

Laguna Beach City Parks and Other Sports Facilities

Laguna is a beach city. Therefore, most of their beautiful parks are beach parks.
However, one of their community parks is truly outstanding: Alta Laguna Park. Its location on 'top of the world' allows you a panoramic view of almost 360 degrees over Laguna's Wilderness Parks, the ocean, and the communities in the valleys.
You can enjoy a variety of formal sports activities, and the park is trailhead to Aliso Wood and Canyons Wilderness Park's West Ridge Trail.
The High School tennis courts (670 Park Avenue) are open to the public after school hours, when not in use by the high school; the school swimming pool is open to the public (nominal fee) on a few mornings and evening during the week.

Alta Laguna Park
Rating: ●●●●●
Location/Access: 3300 Alta Laguna Boulevard, Laguna Beach. From Pacific Coast Highway take Park Avenue in central Laguna. A scenic drive will bring you up the hills to Alta

Tennis courts at Alta Laguna Park

Laguna Boulevard, where you turn left. It dead ends right at the park.
Facilities: Restrooms, drinking fountains (even for dogs), picnic tables with a great view, barbecues, top playground.
Alta Laguna Park is also trailhead to hikes in Aliso Wood and Canyons Wilderness Park via West Ridge Trail.

■ Formal Sports Activities
Tennis, Baseball Basketball, Soccer, Golf

Tennis: Six tennis courts in great shape.
Other: Baseball, basketball (half court), soccer.

Aliso Creek Golf Course

Aliso Creek Golf Course
Rating: ●●●●
Location/Access: 31106 PCH. Just off Pacific Coast Highway in South Laguna opposite Aliso Creek Beach.
Profile: A nine hole course in a beautiful canyon setting, framed by towering walls. No driving range, discount rates available.

Laguna Coast Wilderness Park
Rating: ●●●●◖
Location: Laguna Coast Wilderness Park is located in the San Joaquin Hills between the cities of Laguna Beach, Laguna Hills, Irvine and Newport Beach.
Access: There are many ways to enter the park. There is an entrance to the park that is not far from the beaches in North Laguna. Take San Joaquin Street towards the hills, turn right on Hillcrest Drive and then left on Dartmoor Street. Drive to the end of Dartmoor and park here.
Profile: The 6000 acres of the park are connected to Crystal Cove State Park and to Aliso Wood and Canyons Wilderness Park.
All together the South Coast Wilderness Area covers eighteen thousand acres. Laguna Coast Wilderness Park's trails permit many activities in a great surrounding with stunning views of the Pacific Ocean and of the mountains.
Horseback riding and mountain biking are limited to certain areas.

■ Trail Activities
Hiking, Jogging, Horseback Riding, Mountain Biking

Trip 1: Dartmoor Loop
Hiking

Rating: ●●●●◖
Best Time: Cool season or early morning hours; most of the trail is exposed to the sun.
Distance: 4.7 miles.
Difficulty: Moderate to strenuous; eight hundred feet elevation gain.

Dartmoor Loop Hike

Special Features: This is not only a nature trip but it also demonstrates the diverse architecture of Laguna Beach heading back from Lookout Drive to Dartmoor Drive which is about one and a half miles of urban experience.

The Hike: Walk through the gate and start going up Boat Spur Trail which takes you up seven hundred feet to Guna Peak outlook. Enjoy the panorama of the hills and the coastline; continue on Boat Road going further up.

A quarter and a mile ahead you will reach another intersection. Turn right at Bommer Ridge. Follow it for a short distance and turn right on Water Tank Road. There is another gate which takes you to the end of Lookout Drive and Poplar Street. Walk Poplar Street down to High Street, where you turn right. Follow High Street to Hillcrest Drive, turn right and again right on Dartmoor in order to reach your car.

Trip 2: Laurel Canyon/Willow Canyon Loop
Running, Hiking

Rating: ●●●●●
Distance: 3.7 miles
Difficulty: Mostly easy with some steep uphills.
Best Time: Cool season, early morning.

Access: Park on Laurel Canyon parking lot, Laguna Canyon Road, 1000 feet south of El Toro Road and Laguna Canyon Road intersection. When going south, after you pass Anneliese's Preschool pull into parking on the right (fee).

The Run: At the trailhead adjacent to the parking lot turn right onto Laurel Canyon paralleling Laguna Canyon Road initially. Soon the trail veers off to the left leaving behind traffic noise and other signs of civilization.

This section is one of our favorites because of the diverse nature and feeling of remoteness so close to urban life. The trail gently meanders through a tree dotted meadow with interesting rock formations on the side. After about a mile you start ascending, sometimes steeply, crossing a creek bed. The creek runs water during the rainy season.

After 1.8 miles you reach an intersection. Keep left hiking or jogging up the hill. After half a mile you face another intersection where you turn left again entering Willow Canyon Trail. Willow Canyon offers nice views over the canyons and takes you back to the parking lot.

Trip 3: Phillips Lane into Aliso and Wood Canyons Wilderness Park
Running, Hiking

Running in Laguna Coast Widerness Park

Hiking in Laguna Coast Wilderness Park

Rating: ●●●●
Distance: 3.5 miles.
Difficulty: Moderate to strenuous.
Best Time: Cool season or early morning.
Access: Going south on Laguna Canyon Road coming from the 405 Freeway, pass El Toro Road. Shortly after, Phillips Lane comes up on the left. Limited parking is on Laguna Canyon Road, or on Sun Valley Drive. From Laguna Canyon Road turn left on Hillies Lane, the next road after Phillips Lane, then turn left again on Sun Valley Drive. Park and start you climb up the mountain taking Phillips Lane.

The Hike: At first, you move on pavement which soon gives way to a challenging trail veering to the left at a water tank. The trail is called Stair Steps. However, there's no sign at the bottom of the trail, just on the top. Stair steps indeed! Brace yourself for this narrow, steep, stair step like path with rocks and washed out sections which requires excellent condition.

It takes about twenty minutes of strenuous uphill walking.

At the top turn right on West Ridge Trail which is part of the Laguna Coast Wilderness Park. Follow it, until you reach Top of the World trail. Watch out! West Ridge Trail is frequently used by mountain bikers. The trail basically follows a ridgeline with some steep inclines. To reach the top allow about thirty minutes. Enjoy the view over the ocean, Laguna Beach and the wilderness; return the same way. On this route you can bring your dog. Water is provided at Top of the World Trail. Don't miss Stair Steps on your way back which turns off left from West Ridge Trail. Watch your step going down!

Modification: Hike. Use the same entry. Instead of turning right at West Ridge Trail turn left until you reach Lynx Trail. Descend on Lynx Trail through coastal sage scrub while enjoying views over the canyon.

After seven hundred feet of gentle elevation

Biking in Laguna Coast Wilderness Park

Access: From Interstate 405 exit 133 Laguna Canyon Road and head south for 3.5 miles. Turn right into parking at Nix Nature Center/James Dilley Greenbelt Preserve. Another parking lot to access the trails on the southeast side of the park comes up on the left, four miles south of Interstate 405 just before the 73 Toll Road. The Preserve can also be accessed directly from a parking lot at the intersection of 73 Toll Road and 133 Laguna Canyon Road.

Profile: Nix Nature Center and three new wilderness trails were recently opened to the public. Check with the center. So far, two trails combine with other trails of Laguna Wilderness Park. One trail leads down an underpass to the other side of the canyon road to access Orange County's only natural lake.

Facilities: Restrooms, water.

■ Trail Activities
Hiking, Jogging

drop you join Wood Canyon Trail and head south/right. Walk along the creek. The trail is mostly covered by oaks and other trees. Take a detour following Wood Creek Trail which winds through the oaks paralleling Wood Canyon Trail. You will escape the mountain bikers for one half mile. Then rejoin Wood Canyon.

Hike back up to the ridge taking Rock-It Trail. Rock-It can be steep and rocky, but you can enjoy beautiful vistas. Beware of mountain bikers who might zoom down the trail. When you reach the top, turn right/north until you reach Stair Steps on your left.

Laguna Coast Wilderness Park II - Inland Area
Rating: ●●●●◖
Best time: Year round.
Location: 18751 Laguna Canyon Road, Laguna Beach, Little Sycamore and Nix Nature Center.

Trip 1: Little Sycamore
Hiking, Jogging

Rating: ●●●●
Distance: 4.9 miles.
Difficulty: Easy to moderate.
Best Time: Cool season, early morning hours.
Access: Start at Nix Nature Center, see ppxxx
Special Features: Visit Nix Nature Center which displays an array of educational exhibits covering the canyon's history, American Indian's culture, fossils and rendering of landscapes. The environmentally designed center opened its doors in 2007.
The Trip: From Nix Nature Center head north and find Little Sycamore Trail. At first it follows the valley providing lush vegetation and some shade. At about three quarters of a mile the trail starts to ascend steeply until you reach Serrano Ridge with an elevation of five hundred feet. Turn left and follow the ridge, enjoying a magnificent panorama.

After about one and a half mile turn left on

Little Sycamore Trail with Nix Nature Center in background

Camarillo Canyon Road. Be careful, the descent can be slippery and steep. The trail levels out and you get closer to Laguna Canyon Road. However, there is no trail going straight to the center. You need to turn left on Stagecoach South Trail which takes you up into the hills again until you finally descend to Nix Nature Center. This loop is very enjoyable and diverse. Sorry, no bikes, for hikers only.

Trip 2: Canyon Trail to Barbara's Lake
Loop
Hiking, Jogging

Rating: ●●●●
Distance: 3.9 miles.
Difficulty: Mostly easy.
Best Time: Cool season, early morning hours.
Access: Parking lot at the intersection of south side Laguna Canyon Road and 73 Toll Road.
The Trip: Follow the signs for Canyon Trail and hike through a beautiful meadow dotted with ancient oaks. After about one mile the trail ascends to a ridge called Edison. Turn left down

to Barbara's Lake. Follow the banks of the lake and take the Lake Trail which ends in Back to Parking Lot Trail.

This is a short hike offering beautiful vistas.
Special Features: Lake Barbara, artwork displayed along the banks of the lake.

Canyon Trail to Barbara's Lake Loop

Aliso Wood and Canyons Wilderness Park

Rating: ●●●●●
Best Time: Cooler seasons or early morning.
Location: 28373 Alicia Parkway, Laguna Niguel.
Access: If you take I 5 exit Alicio Parkway, head towards the ocean for approximately five miles. The park entrance is located one hundred yards south of Aliso Creek Road off Alicia Parkway on AWMA Road in the City of Laguna Niguel. The park is bordered by Laguna Beach to the west, Laguna Niguel to the east and Aliso Viejo to the north.
Profile: The Park offers over thirty miles of official trails. It encompasses about 4,000 acres of oaks, sycamores and elderberry trees, scenic canyons, rock formations, two year-round creeks, a fresh water marsh, and a historic landmark, the Dripping Cave, which was a hideout of cattle thieves.
Deer, coyote, bobcats, as well as migratory and native birds and reptiles can be observed.
Facilities: Portable restrooms.
Other Attractions: Orange County Natural History Museum offers exhibits from the local area and gives information on the park's wildlife.
For the Hungry and Thirsty: Either enjoy a picnic in the park, drinks and food snacks are sold at the gift shop in the Natural History Museum, or visit the shopping center off Alicia Parkway and find small restaurants and cafes.

■ Trail Activities

Hiking, Mountain Biking, Equestrian

Trip 1: Aliso Wood Park Loop Mountain Biking (hiking XXL exceeding 2.5 hours).

Rating: ●●●●◖
Distance: Nine miles.
Difficulty: Easy to strenuous.
Best Time: Winter and spring; early morning hours in summer.
Access: From the Interstate 5 take Alicia Parkway south. After you cross Aliso Creek Road, Awna Road comes up on the right.
Park in the street (free) or in the wilderness park parking lot (fee). This is the main trailhead of Aliso and Wood Canyons Wilderness Park.

Wild Hyacinth, Little Sycamore Trail   Aliso Wood Park Loop

The Trip: Follow the paved AWMA Road until a small nature center marks the turn off point to the dirt roads into the park. Turn right on Wood Canyon Trail. You will pass picturesque sand stone rock formations, dense vegetation and cross a creek. Wood Canyon Trail meanders along the valley without much incline. Continue until you come close to a gate at one of the park exits and take up Cholla Trail turning left. Only an experienced mountain biker will be able to bike up Cholla since it's very steep. At the top you reach West Ridge Trail of Laguna Coast Wilderness Park where you turn left.

As you are up on a ridge you have a view of Soka University, which you passed at the bottom on Wood Canyon Trail, of Laguna Beach and the ocean, and the encroaching suburbia from all sides.

Continue on West Ridge Trail which is used by mountain bikers and hikers alike, until you reach your turn off, Mathis Trail. Mathis Trail takes you back down in a long and steep descend to Wood Canyon Trail on which you turn right. From there, take the same way back.

Trip 2: Wood Canyon – Hiking, Jogging

Rating: ●●●●●
Distance: Six miles.
Difficulty: Easy
Best Time: Any
Access: From the 405 Freeway take Irvine Center South which becomes Moulton Parkway. Turn right on Glenwood Drive and right on Canyon Vistas. Drive to the bottom of the hill and park. Walk through the city park, Canyon View Park and reach the trailhead after you pass through gate 7.
Special Features: Dripping Cave and Cave Rock.
The Trip: Walk Wood Canyon Trail which slightly descends. (The first part of the trail is also for mountain bikers.) After you pass Lynx Trail turn right on Wood Creek Trail, which is for hikers only. As the name indicates the trail

Biking on West Ridge Treail in Also Park

runs parallel to Wood Creek which carries water year round. Dense riparian vegetation lines the creek and gives shelter to many animals. Often you will be able to spot deer. This part of the trip is enchanting as it takes you away from civilization into beautiful nature.

After about one and a half miles you reach an intersection with Mathis Trail. Turn right on Mathis and after a few hundred feet turn left on Dripping Cave Trail. Follow the trail and find Dripping Cave, which was a hide out for stagecoach and cattle thieves in the nineteenth century. You can still see some peg holes in the rock from the former users of the cave.

Continue for a quarter of a mile and reach Wood Canyon Trail again and continue. Soon after, turn right for one more sightseeing detour to

Cave Rock, a sand stone rock formation hollowed out by wind and rain. Climbing the various rocks and hiding in the caves provides fun for children and adults alike. Return to Wood Canyon Trail and either follow it back to your starting point or reverse your steps following the same trails as hiking out.

Trip 3: Meadow Loop – Hiking, Mountain Biking

Rating: ●●●●◖
Distance: Five miles.
Difficulty: Moderate
Best Time: Cooler season, early morning.
Access: From the 405 Freeway take the 133 Highway/Laguna Canyon Road south all the

California Poppies in spring

Hiking Meadow Loop

way to PCH and turn left. Turn left on Laguna Avenue which becomes Park Avenue.
Take Park Avenue all the way up the hill until it ends. Turn right on Alta Laguna Boulevard until it loops to the left and park before Top of the World Drive turns off to the right.
Facilities: At Alta Laguna Park – rest rooms, water fountains (even for dogs), picnic tables with a great view, nice playground.
The Trip: Find a small path leading you around Aliso Water Management Agency to a paved road which is the extension of Top of the World Drive called ASWUT Trail and situated in Aliso and Wood Canyons Wilderness Park.
Follow the road for about one quarter of a mile and then turn left on Meadows Trail which is a single trail. Meandering down into the valley offering splendid views, enjoy your hike down into the park. This section is particularly beautiful in spring time when thousands of wildflowers dot the meadows.
Eventually you reach the New AWMA Access Road. Don't turn right as this part of the park is not open to the public. Instead stay on your trail going left paralleling the road until you reach Wood Canyon Trail where you turn left. Follow Wood Canyon, then start the climb by taking Mathis Trail turning left. Beware of mountain bikers, who zip around the bends.
At the top turn left on West Ridge Trail and again enjoy sweeping views over the parks, Laguna Beach and the ocean. Soon you will reach Alta Laguna Park, where you can enjoy a picnic or just rest.
From here take the adjoining street, Alta Laguna Boulevard, for about one mile to get back to your car.

Laguna Niguel Regional Park

One third of the land in Laguna Niguel, neighbor to Laguna Beach, is designed as open space. Laguna Niguel Regional Park, and Salt Creek Regional Park are located in this area. The headquarters of Aliso and Wood Canyons

Around the lake in Laguna Niguel Regional Park

Regional Park, which is for the greater part located in the Laguna Beach are in Laguna Niguel.

Rating: ●●●●(
Best Time: All year.
Location: 28241 La Paz Road, Laguna Niguel
Access: From Toll Road 73 or Interstate 5 exit La Paz Road. Go south for four miles. The park comes up on your right hand side.
From PCH take Crown Valley Parkway to La Paz Road. Proceed north on La Paz. The park is on your left hand side. If you want to avoid the parking fee, walk or ride your bike to the park.
Profile: This 236 acreage of park, of which sixty-five acres are covered with eucalyptus, acacia, white alder, California sycamore, and fir trees is nestled in the Laguna hills. A forty-four acre lake adds to its scenic beauty.
The park offers a variety of trail activities as well as more formal sports activities like tennis

and volleyball. A sports park borders Laguna Niguel Regional Park.
This park is an ideal venue for a family outing, since trails are easy and rather short, and you can combine many of the activities here, for all sites are close to each other. Dogs are permitted, but must be kept on a leash.
Facilities: Restrooms, drinking fountains, playgrounds. Picnic areas equipped with shelters, sinks, barbecues and electric outlets.
Special Features: You can reserve the picnic sites. Our choice is the small shelter number ten up on the hill, where you overlook the park.
For the Hungry and Thirsty: Bring a picnic.

■ Trail Activities
Walking, Biking, Jogging, Horseback Riding

Trip: Around the Lake and up the Hill
Biking, Hiking

Picnic shelter, Laguna Niguel Park

Rating: ●●●◖
Distance: Three miles.
Difficulty: Easy
Best Time: Any time during the week.
The Trip: You cannot get lost here. Mostly paved trails meander through the park. Choose your route either clockwise or counterclockwise around the lake. Bike up the short somewhat steep hill. Have your picnic up here. Return. Combine your trail activity with a more formal sports activity in the park or in the neighboring sports park.

Tennis courts, Laguna Niguel Park

■ Formal Sports Activities
Volleyball, Tennis, Lap Swimming, Other

Volleyball: Two sand volleyball courts.
Tennis: Four very well kept tennis courts. Horseshoe pits.
Other: Baseball and soccer fields in the the neighboring sports park.
Lap Swimming: Swimming in the lake is not permitted. However, there is a heated pool with diving boards in beautiful Crown Valley Community Park at 9751 Crown Valley Parkway, a five minutes drive from the park, if you take La Paz road to Crown Valley Parkway.

Sailing school at Dana Point Harbor

General Area Dana Point

→ **Salt Creek County Beach and Bluff Park**
→ **Salt Creek Trail**
→ **Dana Point Harbor**
→ **Bluff Top Trail, Heritage Park**
   and Lantern Bay Park
→ **Doheny State Beach**
→ **City Parks and Other Public Sports**
   Facilities

www.danapoint.org
dohenystatebeach.org

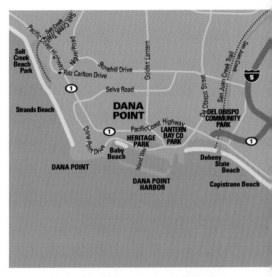

Orientation:

Dana Point is one of those coastal communities which have lost some of their original charm from too much coastal development.

The city is named after the Bostonian Richard Henry Dana, who as a student took a leave of absence from academic life and worked aboard "The Pilgrim" sailing to California around Cap Horn in 1835. There, the crew loaded dried cattle skin (California banknotes) in exchange for goods it brought to the San Juan Capistrano Mission.

Since there was no harbor in existence, the hides were thrown from the rugged cliffs that backed the cove, down to the beach at what is now called Dana Point. In his famous autobiographical book of 1840 "Two Years Before the Mast", Dana called the cove the "only romantic place" in California.

Later, the great swells at the cove made it a surfer's paradise, which was destroyed by the construction of a jetty, a yacht harbor and a harbor side community in the early 1970s.

At this artificially made yacht harbor you find walkways for a leisurely stroll as well as opportunities to swim or launch your kayak, or to explore tide pools at its northern end.

Rugged Cliffs at Dana Point's north coast

View from Heritage Park to south

On top of the Cliffs that frame the harbor, are Heritage Park, Bluff Top Trail, and Lantern Bay Park, which all are great for walking and viewing the harbor and the coast, particularly nice at sunset.

In the northern part of Dana Point there is Salt Creek County Beach and Bluff Park, which is a great area with a large sandy beach, very much favored by locals and visitors alike.

Doheny State Beach south of the harbor is another jewel of Orange County's beaches. However, it has also been affected by the urban development of Dana Point.

The former challenging surf there has been calmed to an extent, that skilled surfers felt like they have lost their paradise; however, less experienced surfers and swimmers now enjoy the calmer waters of Doheny State Beach.

Camino Capistrano Beach Park is the continuation of Doheny State Beach to the south. It stretches for miles along Pacific Coast Highway, unfortunately, a little too close to the highway.

From the twenty-three city parks, the largest of them, Del Obispo Park, is most attractive to physically active persons. It offers opportunities for a variety of more formal sports like basketball and tennis.

A nice hiking and biking trail starts at the Pacific Ocean. It runs along the Salt Creek riverbed and then along Salt Creek Park up to Chapparosa Park in the foothills of the Santa Ana Mountains.

San Juan Capistrano Beach Park

Active at Salt Creek County Beach

Salt Creek County Beach and Bluff Park

Rating: ●●●●◖
Best Time: All Year.
Location: 33333 South Pacific Coast Highway. Dana Point between the north end of Dana Point and South Laguna.
Access: There are two ways of getting to the beach. Both are off Pacific Coast Highway. The

Strands Beach/Selva Beach in Dana Point

popular way is to turn into Ritz Carlton Drive and then into the large parking lot (fee).

You walk through an underpass and then a couple of hundred yards down along the greens of the Bluff Park to the wide and almost two miles long beach which is divided by the Ritz Carlton on top of the bluffs into a southern and northern part.

The second access is via Selva Road off PCH towards the coast and then into a large metered parking lot. As an alternative, you can also park there in the street for free. Walk down the long winding path that also has several steps to the south side of Salt Creek Beach, which is also called Strands Beach or Selva Beach. Additionally, you can also use the new elevator cabin to get down to the beach.

Profile: There are 18 acres of public beach at this location. The northern area is wide and is covered with fine white sand. The grassy Bluff Park has all the amenities which you might find appealing, which is why the young and families prefer it.

Competitor at Salt Creek Beach

Near the southern ramp at Strands the sand can disappear at high tide (see image previous page). At the south end close to the framing bluffs, the sandy area is rather wide again, even during high surf. We have always preferred the southern part, because it is more remote. But land above the southern bluffs has been developed; some of its serene character is lost. Instead there is now a cement walkway below the development above the beach.

Facilities: Rest rooms, showers, water fountains, picnic tables, barbecue grills, life guards at the northern part of the beach.

Rest rooms, showers, water fountains by the parking lot on top of the bluffs at the southern part of the beach.

For the Hungry and Thirsty: In spring and summer you can buy snacks at the concession stands at the northern part of Salt Creek Beach. Of course, if you want to be fancy, you can also have a snack or meal on top of the bluffs at the Ritz Carlton overlooking the beach.

■ Water Activities
Swimming, Boogie Boarding, Surfing, SUP

Swimming: The surf is more often strong here. Even though the sand is very level where it meets the water, the surf breaks close to shore which may cause problems for children and less experienced swimmers.

The water usually gets an A rating.

Surfing competition at Salt Creek Beach

Salt Creek Beach, viewing north

Boogie Boarding, Surfing, SUP: Just north of the Ritz Carlton area, surfing is great (surfing competitions are held here), since a small reef generate good swells here.

Further north the surf comes in evenly, so that area can be recommended also for less experienced persons and for kids with boogie boards.

■ Trail Activities
Walking, Jogging

Trip: Salt Creek Beach and Bluff Top Park Loop
Walking, Running

Rating: ●●●●(
Distance: Up to 3.5 miles.
Difficulty: Easy, since the sand at the beach is firm.
Best Time: All year mornings and early evenings at lower tide.

The Trip: Starting point is the parking lot at Selva Road. Go down the ramp and walk (run) north along the southern part of the beach, continue walking (running) to the northern end of the beach near Monarch Bay, turn back. About half way back take the small path up to the walkway at the Bluff Park, where you will find a rest room; continue south until you enter the path that goes up to the bluff top at the Ritz

Runnig along the shore at Salt Creek Beach

The final steps of Salt Creek Trail hike

Carlton. It is public, and you will enjoy great vistas of the coastline and Catalina Island. Also in winter you might catch sight of migrating whales.

There are quite a bit of benches, where you can rest, if you feel the need. Then descend the same way, turn south, and walk (or run) to the ramp that brings you back to the parking lot.

Modification 1: Continue south until the southern border of the park, turn around and continue north again until you are back at the ramp. This variation adds another three quarter of a mile to your trip.

Modification 2 : The walk gets a little shorter, if you start from the parking lot at the Ritz Carlton Drive, going through the gate at the Ritz Carlton that is open to the public. It leads you around the hotel to the cliff top overview path, which you walk down.

Continue on the beach to the north as described above. On your way back through the Bluff Top Park continue until you hit the ramp to the parking lot. Walk up the ramp to where you parked your car.

■ Formal Sports Activities
Basketball, Volleyball, Golf

Basketball: One half court in Bluff Park.
Volleyball: Nets on the beach.
Golf: Monarch Bay Golf Course (inland right behind Salt Creek Beach and Bluff Park).

Salt Creek Trail
Hiking, Biking

Trip: Salt Creek Trail Hike
Rating: ●●●●◖
Best Time: Spring, winter, and fall.
Difficulty: Easy, a few tricky turns if you bike.
Distance: Four miles roundtrip to Clubhouse Plaza Shopping Center (hiking), six miles to Chapparosa Community Park (biking).
Profile: This hike or bike ride through Salt Creek Canyon, goes along the Salt Creek bed and connects the beach with the inland hills east of PCH up to Chapparosa Park in Laguna Niguel.
Facilities: See Salt Creek beach hike.

Chapparosa Park facilities: drinking fountain, rest rooms, picnic tables, barbecues, play area.
The Trip: When we hike, we are not sure, which way is more fun: to start from the beach and hike up Salt Creek Canyon first, or start from the shopping center and hike down to the beach.

After you park our car at the shopping center, you turn right next to the Italian Restaurant and follow the path uphill alongside Salt Creek Canyon.

Even though you hike to the beach, you will encounter some uphill ascends, before you slowly descend. The view of Creek Canyon is especially rewarding in spring, when after winter rains plants are blooming.

To reach the underpass at Camino del Avion, you turn left right before the highway and follow this only small unpaved portion of the path to the underpass.

Next you will hike about a mile along the west side of Monarch Beach Golf Course, before another underpass gets you to the other side of Pacific Coast Highway. You keep to the left - the golf course is now at your right – and after a few dozen yards you reach Bluff Park and the beach is all yours.

You can either descend right away to the sands, or walk along the promenade to the grassy area or you can take the path that leads up to the Ritz Carlton overview.

Viewing inland from Salt Creek Trail

Monarch Bay Golf Course from Salt Creek Trail

Have a good swim and a picnic afterwards. Return the same way.

Modification (Biking): The biking trip is best from Salt Creek Beach parking lot. Follow the path down to the grassy area, turn right at the promenade, and ride north parallel to the beach. At the golf course the path takes a right turn and leads you right to the underpass through PCH. Watch out for golf carts there. Continue and you will have the golf course to your right. The distant hills and Salt Creek Canyon beyond the golf course make a great picture.

Almost half way to Camino del Avion, there is a dangerous place for speedy cyclists, since erosion has damaged the trail. You are supposed to walk your bike there, but that sign is often overlooked.

The final part up to Niguel Road (where the shopping center is) is first a gentle uphill, before

View toward Ocean from Salt Creek Trail

it ends with a downhill slope. (You can have a snack at one of the shopping center's eateries). Use the underpass to get to the other side of Niguel Road. Continue through San Juan Canyon Sulphur Creek Canyon and Salt Creek Regional Park to Chapparosa Community Park, your final destination and turning point.

Special Features: Along the promenade in Bluff Park, there are benches, which invite you to sit down and watch for whales during the migrating season or enjoy views of Catalina Island and the coastline.

For The Hungry and Thirsty: There is a café, a juice bar, and an Italian Restaurant at the Clubhouse Shopping Center. There is also a concession stand by the Salt Creek Bluff Park (seasonal); picnic tables are at Chapparosa Park.

Dana Point Harbor

Rating: ●●●●, for swimming ●●●
Best Time: All year.
Location/Access: From Pacific Coast Highway turn into Golden Lantern, then turn into Santa Clara, then left into Ensenada Place-Heritage Park. There is a huge parking lot by the harbor.
Profile: If you are not familiar with the old Dana Point the yacht harbour will seem quite nice, a good place for boating, and an opportunity for a walk or a swim.
Facilities: Restrooms, showers, drinking fountain, life guards seasonally (at Baby Beach)
For the Hungry and Thirsty: There are many restaurants at Dana Point Harbor. We like casual

Baby Beach at Dana Point Harbor

Dana Point Harbor

Jon's Fish Market on Golden Lantern right at the shore on the south side of the harbor. You can eat outside. They also sell fresh fish.

■ Water Activities
Swimming, SUP, Sailing

Swimming: There are two small beaches within the northern harbor area:
Baby Beach, a calm water beach that sits underneath towering cliffs. It is often recommended for families with small children. Since the waters of yacht harbors are often polluted, we cannot recommend it for small children, even though it is very safe, and the scenery around it is quite pleasant.
The other tiny beach is just the opposite of Baby Beach. The waters are very rough here. You find it at Harbor Point, right after you pass the Ocean Institute and walk through the cage, which protects from falling rocks. The coast here looks

how it might have been during Dana's time. This beach is framed by tidepools and rocks. Swimming is recommended for experts only.
Boating: You can launch your kayak, canoe or SUP here, since the beach is close to the parking lot. Explore the harbor, or the harbor channel,

Stand up paddeling at Dana Point Harbor

Walkway on cliff edges on top of Dana Point Harbor

or venture out to the ocean. There is also a sailing school at the harbor.

SUP: In the calm waters of the harbour you can practise the new sport of stand up paddeling.

■ Trail Activities

Walking

Heritage Park, Bluff Top Trail, Lantern Bay County Park
Walking

Rating: ●●●●
Difficulty: Easy to moderate.
Best Time: All year.
Distance: Trip 1: 2.5 miles, trip 2: four miles.
Location/Access: Heritage Park: 34400 Old Golden Lantern off PCH. Bluff TopTrail: Trail access (from Pacific Coast Highway) is either at Violet Lantern and El Camino Capistrano or at Amber Lantern and Santa Clara.

Lantern Bay Park: 25111 Dana Point Harbor Drive. However, best access is via Park Lantern up the bluffs. Street parking is free.

Trip 1: Bluff Top Trail (Roundtrip)
Walking

Follow the trail along the cliffs; once a while you cross a wooden bridge in front of the mansions. Enjoy the unique vistas.

Trip 2: Heritage Park/Lantern Bay Park
Walking

Follow the meandering trail through Heritage Harbor Park. It takes you to several view points. Walk down to Dana Point Harbor Drive. Follow it; cross Golden Lantern and enter Heritage Park. Walk along the cliffs. The park is famous for its ocean view. Walk down Park Lantern all the way to Doheny State Beach. Enjoy the Pacific Ocean, perhaps take a swim and return to where you parked.

Doheny State Beach

Rating: ●●●●
Best Times: Late spring, summer and fall.
Location: Dana Point Harbor Drive in South Dana Point.
Access: From Pacific Coast Highway turn into Dana Point Harbor Drive. The Park entrance is on your left. There is ample parking (fee) close to the sand.
There is also a special wheelchair access ramp. If you turn right into Park Lantern and drive up the hill to Lantern Park, you can park free in the street.
Profile: The popular beach (over two million visitors per year) is wide, sandy, and has one of the warmest waters in Orange County. The vicinity of Pacific Coast Highway makes access easy, but can also cause noise. There are two day use areas and a large camping area for tents and trailers close to the beach.

■ Water Activities
Swimming, Surfing, Boogie Boarding, SUP, Scuba Diving, Snorkeling, Boating

Swimming: The sand is level, where it meets the water, which makes this beach a favorite for families with small children and for inexperienced swimmers. Water quality is usually good; sometimes however, the rating can be lower than A. (Check the local newspaper).
Surfing: Due to the harbor and the jetties, the surf is gentle at Doheny Beach, which generally makes it a heaven for less experienced surfers; however, if a south swell emerges, even the real surfers return.
SUP: More and more stand up paddlers frequent Doheny State Beach.
Boogie Boarding: Youngsters enjoy the gentle surf.
Scuba Diving. Snorkeling: Dohenny State Beach is not the greatest place for these activities, but you can do them here.
Boating: Doheny Beach is also good for launching your man powered boat, since parking is close to the water. There are no hidden rocks, and the surf is hardly ever a problem.

■ Trail Activities
Walking, Jogging, Biking, Inline Skating

You can walk, hike or jog right down by the water. The sand is firm, which makes it a little easier on the muscles. Choose your own distance and turning point, since the sand stretches for miles beyond Doheny through Capistrano Beach, all the way to San Clemente.
Biking, Inline Skating: A bike path runs along Doheny State Beach and continues through

Doheny State Beach

Gentle surf at Doheny Beach draws children

On a snorkeling trip

Capistrano Beach, then becomes a bicycle path along PCH which turns into Camino Capistrano. You can go all the way to San Clemente Pier with your bike.

Inline Skaters have to turn at Estancia. Bikers continue on the unpaved City Beach Trail in San Clemente and continue to San Clemente Pier (fourteen miles round trip, XXL).

▓ Formal Sports Activities
Basketball, Volleyball

Basketball: South of Doheny State Beach, at Capistrano Beach one basketball court.

Volleyball: Six volleyball nets by the beach in the day use area of Doheny Beach State Park.

Combo: Doheny State Beach is another of Orange County Beach Parks that allows for many different activities, enabling anyone to find his or her optimal combination.

You can inline skate before you swim, or play volleyball or basketball, or jog, hike, bike or walk first along the beach before you swim.

Dana Point City Parks and Public Sports Facilities

Profile: Dana Point is also a beach community. Therefore, most of its parks are somehow connected to beach activities or viewing the beach. In the following we will only introduce Del Obispo Park below, since it is the largest of Dana Point city parks and offers facilities for a variety of sports activities.

Dana Point Tennis Center, provides excellent facilities for tennis at minimal cost.

▓ Formal Sports Activities
Tennis, Basketball, Baseball

Del Obispo Park
Rating: ●●●◖
Location: 34052 Del Obispo Street.
Access: Off PCH turn inland at Del Obispo

Del Obispo Park

Dana Point Tennis Center

Mission San Juan Capistrano ruins

Street. After a few blocks turn right into the parking lot (free).
Facilities: Restrooms, picnic tables, barbecue grills, playground.
Tennis: Two courts in very good condition.
Basketball: One well-kept court.
Baseball: One field.

Dana Point Tennis Center
Rating: ●●●●
Location: 24911 Calle de Tennis
Access: From PCH drive inland on Golden Lantern, turn right into Calle de Tennis. Parking is free.
Tennis: There are eight championship tennis courts, rentable for a nominal fee.

Other Attractions: The Ocean Institute at 25111 Dana Point Harbor Drive is a non-profit educational center offering diverse programs. There is a Visitor Center and an Aquarium at Doheny State Beach.
Famous Mission San Juan Capistrano is about a fifteen minutes drive inland. It is definitely worth a side trip. See the San Juan Capistrano chapter.
For the Hungry and Thirsty: There are concession stands right at Doheny State Beach. If you camp at Doheny State Beach, you can buy the fresh fish at Jon's Fish Market (see p. 130/131). Prepare your fish meal yourself; then enjoy your meal at the picnic area at Doheny State Beach.

Access ramp to San Clemente State Beach

General Location San Clemente

→ **San Clemente City Beach**
→ **Calafia Beach Park**
→ **San Clemente State Beach**
→ **San Clemente City Parks and other Public Sports Facilities**

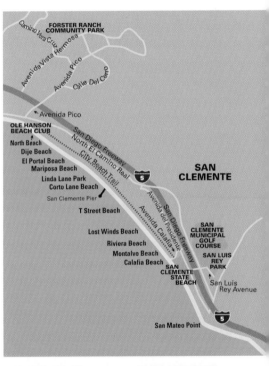

www.ci.san-clemente.ca.us
www.parks.gov

Orientation:

Half way between Los Angeles and San Diego you will find one of the most charming towns in Orange County, San Clemente.

Founder of the city Ole Hansen envisioned it as a "Spanish Village by the Sea", with white houses and red tile roofs. It has somehow preserved its small town setting and its casual atmosphere. Many of the houses here sit on top of the weathered bluffs that closely line the Pacific almost throughout the most southern community of Orange County.

Ravines that cut through the rugged cliffs here and there make for easier access to the ocean. Its beautiful sandy beach (each part has its own name) stretches all the way from where El Camino hits the ocean near Ole Hansen Beach Club, in the north to San Clemente State Beach in the south. It continues to San Mateo Point, a surfer's paradise, which also marks the boundary between Orange and San Diego Counties.

The over three hundred sunny days and the year round mild climate make this city a perfect spot for the outdoor activist, and especially for the water sports enthusiast.

San Clemente City Beach near the pier

The coastline from San Clemte State Beach, viewing north

The many active city parks permit the person who prefers more formal sports, to play baseball, basketball, soccer, and tennis among others in a very scenic setting. Forster Ranch Community Park up in the hills seems the most inviting for the active person.

The municipal golf course, adjacent to San Luis Rey Park provides ocean views.

For hikers, joggers and bikers the city also offers special multi-use trails, above all the Beach Coastal Trail, as well as Forster Ranch Ridgeline Trail (see p. 146) and Rancho San Clemente Ridgeline Trail inland for hiking.

San Clemente City Beach

Rating: ●●●●◑
Best Time: Late spring, summer and fall.
Location: City of San Clemente, north and south of the pier, a little over a mile in each direction.

Access: There are numerous access paths to San Clemente City Beach.

If you are to visit the pier area, exit Interstate 5 at Camino Real in San Clemente. Drive north on Camino Real, turn West into Avenida del Mar, which leads you right to Parque del Mar and the pier area (municipal parking lot).

San Clemente City Beach, south of the pier

You will find metered street parking at various places, and also five municipal parking lots along City Beach.

At North Beach by the Metrolink Station beach access is provided from Calle Deshecha and Avenue Estacion, off El Camino Real (PCH). There is a large municipal parking lot and also street parking with easy access to the beach.

Dije Beach (204) access is from Dije Court; street parking, long steep stairs.

El Portal Beach access is from El Portal; street parking, long steep paved path.

Mariposa Beach access is from Mariposa; street parking, long steep paved path.

Linda Lane Park access is from Linda Lane; parking lot, stairs.

Corto Lane Trail Crossing; street parking, stairs. South of the pier you will find beach access: T Street Trail Crossing from T Street Overlook Boca del Canon.

Lost Winds Beach from Calle de los Alamos; street parking, steep path.

Riviera Beach, street parking, short stairs from Piazza a la Playa.

Montalvo Beach from Piazza a la Playa; street parking.

Profile: The long municipal beach of San Clemente is mostly straight, where the eroded cliffs that line it get more and more impressive the further you go south.

Train tracks are squeezed between the sands and the cliffs all along San Clemente, and two small train stations sit right by the beach.

Even though in many places the beach is protected from trains by dunes or bushes it is a minor setback to its otherwise great scenery.

Weathered bluffs separate the beach from the busy world up on top, while the yellow sands, and the active surf, which hardly ever comes to a rest here, make it a wonderful place to be active in the open. It is a favorite with young people and families.

Facilities: Restrooms at most beach areas, also lifeguards (seasonal), drinking fountains, showers at the main beach areas.

On the way to a good surfing spot

Other Attractions: The fishing pier downtown, which is another gift from the city's founder Ole Hansen, is a landmark since 1920. It was rebuilt a couple of times after storms destroyed it. Walking it rewards you with another stunning view of southern Orange County's coastline. Casa Romantica (Cultural Center and Gardens), former Ole Hansen's residence, sits up on the bluffs by the pierproviding great views.

For the Hungry and Thirsty: Fisherman's Restaurant, Fissherman's Bar, Beach Garden Cafe (all at Avenida Victoria) right by the beach at the pier; concession stands at Nort Beach and T Street Beach.

■ Water Activities

Swimming, Surfing, Boogie Boarding, Boating

Rating: ●●●●◖

Swimming: The surf is mostly strong along the cost here, but the coast is flat, where it meets the water. Watch children nonetheless.

You will find swimmers at most non-surfing territories, however, they prefer North Beach, the south side of the pier; T Street is safe for smaller folks, since a sandbar creates shallow waters. In the south, swimming is often good at Riviera and Montalve.

Water quality is mostly A, and the beach in general seems well attended.

Surfing: You will find surfers challenging the

San Clemente Pier and downtown

waves north at "204" (offshore reefs), a surfer's beach, at T Street, where there is the most popular and consistent surf break within the city, however, morning surfing only in the summer. A popular surf break exists also north of the pier. Conditions vary here; they can be excellent. In the south surfing is popular between Riviera Beach and Montalvo Beach.

Body Boarding: mostly in typical swimming areas.

Boating: North Beach is a good place for launching your kayak or canoe for open water activity, since parking is rather close to the beach and access is easy.

■ Trail Activities
Walking, Running, Biking

Water Activities dominate in San Clemente. However, since the Beach Coastal Trail was extended, there is a good opportunity for hikers and joggers close to the beach. Biking other then in streets is somewhat limited.
Walking, Hiking and Biking

San Clemente Beach Loop
Walking, (Running, Biking)
Rating: ●●●●◖, for biking ●●●◖
Best Time: All year.
Distance: Four to six miles roundtrip; (modification: eight miles roundtrip).
Difficulty: Easy, if you take the Beach Trail, moderate along the beach, even though there is hardly any elevation gain; the sand on the beach is deep.
Access: You can park at any beach access point (see above). We would recommend either at North Beach, at the parking lot by the pier, at San Clemente State Beach day-use area (see p. 145) or at Calafia Beach.
Facilities: Restrooms, showers, drinking fountains.

Profile: As a beach hike this is one of our favorites in Orange County. For most of your hike, especially the southern part of it, you are protected from the busy and noisy world. You can enjoy the stunning views of the towering cliffs on one side and the never resting ocean and its sea life on the other side.

As a run it is also great fun, whether you choose the water line or the path as your course.

As a bike ride it is almost too short to give you a good workout, since you can use it only to Calafia Beach and would have to walk your bike on the Mariposa Point Boardwalk, and on the asphalt area at the base of the pier.

The Walk: The advantage of starting at the pier area is, having a choice of restaurants waiting for you after you finish your hike.

From the pier to Calafia Beach Park you cover 1.2 miles. The first part close to the pier is on the beach side of the tracks. At T street trail

Running on City Beach Trail

crossing, you will cross to cliff side of the tracks, and hike on this side until you reach Calafia. This part can be somewhat dusty at the end of the dry season. If you hike further on passing San Clemente State Beach Park (which we recommend strongly), you cover another mile.

At the State Beach, walk through the tunnel that protects you from the train tracks, and then up the impressive steep ravine, which connects the beach to the bluff top part of the park and the huge camping area. Enjoy the view that will reach for miles and miles to the south and to the north; in winter, watch for migrating whales. Walk down back to the beach and turn north.

At Calafia Beach Park, you have the choice of either returning the same way you came, or hiking along the City Beach Trail, which runs along the bluffs' base. Back at the pier, enjoy your meal at one of the eateries.

Modification 1 (XXL): If you want to do an XXL walk, continue for another one and a half miles and make Mateo Point and the famous Trestles your turning point. On this stretch of your trip you will meet sea birds only. At Trestle you can watch birds that especially assemble near the creek mouth in winter and admire the expert surfers that are always there. If walking or running through the heavy sand gets too

Walking along San Clemente State Beach

Mariposa Walkway, San Clemente

tiring on your return trip, you can cross the train tracks close to San Clemente State Beach and return using the trail on the foot of the cliffs.

Modification 2: Start your hike at the parking lot of North Beach by the Ole Hansen Beach Club, and walk along the beach for a mile to the pier; however, since part of the way the sands disappear at high tide, this route is

recommended at minus tide only. At the pier follow the route described above. After your meal break near the pier, hike back along the northern part of the San Clemente Beach Trail that includes an 850 foot long elevated walkway at Mariposa Point.

■ Formal Sports Activities
Lap Swimming, Volleyball

Ole Hansen Beach Club
Lap Swimming
The Ole Hanson Beach Club (105 West Avenida Pico) at the north end of the city houses a 25m size swimming pool, where the original "Tarzan" Jonny Weissmuller qualified for the 1928 Olympic swimming competition.

You can use the heated pool for a marginal fee all year. It is close to the ocean.

Get a tan at the beach and exercise in the pool.
Beach Volleyball: On North Beach, by the pier, and near Riviera Beach you find volleyball nets.

Ole Hansen Beach Club

Calafia State Beach Park

Rating: ●●●●◖
Best Time: Late spring, summer and fall.
Location: In south San Clemente at the west end of Avenida Calafia.
Access: Take the Avenida Calafia exit from Interstate 5, if you come from the north. Drive all the way down to the Beach Park. Metered Parking.
If you approach from the south take the Christianitos Road exit off I 5. Turn left, cross the Freeway onto Avenue El Presidente, drive north until Avenida Calafia; turn left and drive down to the beach parking.
Access to the water is easy, just a few steps across the railroad tracks, than to the sand via short stairs.

Boogie Boarders at Calafia State Beach

Profile: This small attractive beach park in between San Clemente City Beach and San Clemente State Beach is by no means different from the City Beach.
Due to its location at the south end of town it is attractive, since it is more remote. The train tracks are close, but trains only zip by occasionally.
Facilities: Restrooms, showers, water fountains.
For the Hungry and Thirsty: Concession stand (seasonal).

■ Water Activities

Swimming, Boogie Boarding, Surfing, Boating

Swimming: There are no hidden rocks in the water; the surf line parallels the beach. So swimming is mostly good; less experienced swimmers should watch out, when the surf gets stronger.
Boogie Boarding: Calafia State Beach is crowded with boogie boarders.
Surfing: You will always find surfers here; however, the quality of surfing depends on the unpredictable swell.
Boating: Since beach access is easy, carrying

Beach fun in the evening sun

San Clemente City Beach Trail, south end

your kayak, canoe or SUP-board to the water is no big job here.

■ Trail Activities
Walking, Hiking, Running

Calafia is a great starting point for your beach walk, hike or a run, either north or south. (See also p. 140). If you go south in the offseason, your only company are seabirds.

Trip: Calafia Beach to Trestles Loop Walk (Run)

Rating: ●●●●◖
Best Time: All year.
Distance: 4.5 miles roundtrip.
Difficulty: Moderate, due to heavy sands.
Facilities: Restrooms, showers, lifeguards (seasonal) and picnic areas.
Profile: You walk, hike or run with the Pacific

to one side and for the most part of the way the rugged sandstone cliffs on the other side.
Other Attractions: Camping in neighboring San Clemente State Beach on top of the bluffs, where you can enjoy a great view.
For the Hungry and Thirsty: Concession stand (seasonal), or bring a picnic.
The Trip: If you head south along the beach after crossing the railroad tracks, you first pass by San Clemente State Beach at the foot of its steep bluffs, then walk (run) along a stretch of beach, where the upper part is private property of the homeowners on top of the cliff. (Up to the medium high tide line it is public, though.) Try to catch a peak of Casa Pacifica, former President Nixon's Western White House, even though part of it is concealed by tall trees.
At your destination Mateo Point, which marks the border between Orange County and San Diego County, rest for a while and watch the birds at the mouth of San Mateo Creek which empties into the Pacific right here.
On your way back, take a detour at San Clemente State Beach if you are still full of energy. Walk up the southern beach access trail, passing through the ravine and enjoying the view from the top.
Take the northern beach access trail down, which leads to the underpass at the train tracks. Continue to Calafia Beach.

Casa Pacifica, San Clemente

San Clemente State Beach

San Clemente State Beach

Rating: ●●●●◐
Best Time: All Year.
Location: South San Clemente, off Calafia Avenue.
Access: From Interstate 5 turn off in San Clemente at Avenida Calafia. Head West about half a mile until the entrance up the hill to the left. You can park for a fee in San Clemente State Beach, or you can drive down Avenida Calafia to Calafia Beach Park, where you will find metered parking. If you want to save your quarters, some free parking is available in neighboring streets. You get to the beach from the park via one of two steep trails through gaps in the cliff walls and an underpass below the tracks or a railroad crossing.
Profile: This mile long beach offers a scenic backdrop of eroded bluffs. However, the beach is narrow at places during high tide, so the railroad tracks can be significantly close to the water. On the top of the bluffs area is a great campground. The top also makes an excellent viewing point.
Facilities: Restrooms, lifeguards (seasonal) and picnic areas.

■ Water Activities
Swimming, Surfing

Swimming: There can be rip currents, and the sand sometimes slopes sharply near the water´s edge. Be careful, if you are not an expert.
If you stay at the park's campground, you should probably go swimming a little further north at the nearby Calafia Beach Park or at Riviera Beach.
Water quality most of the time is rated A.
Surfing: Surfers like the State Beach: however, experts go down to Trestles, which is quite a trip from the park, since it is in San Diego County. Access is also via San Mateo Campground, wherefrom you also have to walk quite a bit.

The Coastline south of San Clemente

Taking a nap on the beach

■ Trail Activities
Walking, Hiking, Jogging, Running

See p. 140, 144 for the various trips, which you can also start from San Clemente State Beach.
Combo: Swimming can be combined with hiking, running or walking.

Special Features: The view atop the bluffs is a dream. San Clemente State Beach also has one of the best coastal camping in California.

San Clemente City Parks and Other Public Sports Facilities

The great thing about San Clemente's city parks is that most of them have ocean view and/or a mountain view, which makes exercising there the more enjoyable. You can either participate in more formal sports activities, like basketball, baseball, softball, soccer, tennis, volleyball and lawn bowling, or walking, or running.

■ Formal Sports Activities
Track Running, Ball Games, Tennis, Basketball, Lawn Bowling, Golf

Forster Ranch Community Park (Pirate's Park)
Rating: ●●●●◖
Location: 3207 Camino Vera Cruz (Tennis), 1291 Calle Sarmentoso.
Access: Take the Avenida Pico exit, turn left into Camino Vera Cruz, turn right into Calle Sarmentoso.
Facilities: Drinking fountain, rest rooms, great playground.
Profile: Even though Forster Ranch Park lies quite a bit inland, it is very popular with the people of San Clemente. It offers many different opportunities to exercise, and the scenery around is great.
You have also access to Forster Ranch Ridgeline Trail, a 3.2 mile long nice trail with great views of the coastline, the community, and the surrounding hills.
Running: The running track is oversized, not in top condition, but anyhow it is great to jog there, because of the tranquillity and the scenic hills surrounding it.
Baseball/Softball, Soccer: Multi-use field.
Tennis: Two well kept tennis courts (lighted).
Basketball: Basketball court.

Forster Ranch Community Park, San Clemente

San Luis Rey Park

Rating: ●●●(, for tennis ●●●●(
Location: 109 Ave San Luis Rey.
Access: From Interstate 5 exit onto Camino Real, turn to Avenue Magdalene, then Calle de Commercio, then Avenue San Luis Rey.
Profile: We chose this small neighborhood park since it is close to San Clemente State Beach, and the municipal golf course is next to it.
It is the only park in South Orange County that offers Lawn Bowling (free).
Tennis: Four lighted courts, in good condition.
Lawn Bowling: If you prefer a less physically demanding activity, this is the place to go to.

San Clemente Municipal Golf Course:

Rating: ●●●●
Location: 150 E. Avenue Magdalena.
Accesss: Coming on I 5, exit onto Camino Real in southern direction, turn left on Avenue Magdalena, and you are almost there.
Profile: For this traditional 1928 built Golf Course the land was also donated by Ole Hansen. The eighteen hole course is open to the public at a very reasonable rate.
Nine hole play on the back nine is permitted in the early morning, when you pay half price.
Walking permitted, driving range.

Tennis at San Luis Rey Park

San Clemente Municipal Golf Course

4.

Activities in Inland Areas

Biking in Chino Hills Park

General Area Yorba Linda

→ **Carbon Canyon Regional Park**
→ **Chino Hills State Park**
→ **Yorba Regional Park**

www.ci.yorba-linda.ca.us
www.ocparks.com

Orientation:

Yorba Linda is a suburban like city in the northeast of Orange County.

The city is noted for its park like setting. It prides itself for its extensive trail system of 100 miles of equestrian, hiking and biking trails, as well as its three public equestrian arenas and its Black Gold Golf Course, which is one of the finest city owned golf courses in the nation.

To the north of Yorba Linda one finds the vast wilderness area of Chino Hills State Park (12,500 acres). A sizeable portion of the park is located within Orange County boundaries, but larger areas stretch into San Bernardino and Riverside Counties. We will cover the western part of the park located in Orange County.

Connected to Chino Hills Park to the northwest is Carbon Canyon Regional Park, the most northern of Orange County's parks.

Opportunities for many outdoor activities in the area can be found at Yorba Regional Park which is located south of Chino Hills State Park at the mouth of Santa Ana Canyon along the banks of the Santa Ana River.

Mountain view from Chino Hills Park

Redwood grove at Carbon Canyon Park

Carbon Canyon Regional Park

Rating: ●●●●
Best time: Any time.
Location: 4442 Carbon Canyon Road, Brea.
Access: From the 55 Freeway going inland take the 91 Freeway towards Riverside. Exit Imperial Highway, turn left/north. Turn right on Valencia Avenue and right on Carbon Canyon Road. Carbon Canyon Regional Park comes up on your right.
Or take Freeway 57 going north. Exit on Lambert Road, turn right. Lambert becomes Carbon Canyon Road. The park is on your right.
Profile: Carbon Canyon Regional Park consists of 124 acres; a grove of some 200 coastal redwoods has been established on ten acres.
Carbon Canyon Regional Park offers many recreational opportunities. Hiking, biking and equestrian trails meander through the park and connect to the trail system of Chino Hills State Park.
Facilities: Barbecues, fire rings, picnic areas, one group shelter (fee), five playgrounds, restrooms, amphitheater.
Special Features: 1.12 mile self-guided nature trail explaining local flora. Interpretive Center with educational programs.
For the Hungry and Thirsty: Picnics are a must at one of the many picnic shelters in the park. Outside the park find Sol de Mexico

Restaurant: Leave Carbon Canyon Park; turn right on Carbon Canyon Road. Go for about 0.5 miles and turn left on Olinda Road. Turn right into the parking lot and find Sol de Mexico restaurant. Enjoy genuine home cooked Mexican food.

▨ Trail Activities
Hiking, Jogging, Mountain Biking, Horseback Riding

Trip 1: Carbon Canyon Loop
Hiking, Jogging

Rating: ●●●◖
Distance: 2.5 miles.
Difficulty: Easy
Best Time: Any time for the 1.12 mile Nature Trail portion. For the remaining part of the loop cooler conditions make it more enjoyable.
The Trip: Find the trailhead past the tennis courts at the east end of the park at a pine grove. Cross Carbon Creek and follow the self-guided Nature Trail which runs mostly parallel to Carbon Creek. Towards the end reach a T-intersection, turn left and find the remarkable redwood grove.
This 200 tree redwood grove is one of a kind in Orange County as redwoods normally don't thrive this far south. Take a rest and enjoy the majestic calm of the trees before you continue passing to the other side of the grove onto a paved path.
Turn right and hike along the Carbon Canyon Creek Dam, which was built from 1959 to 1965. At the north end of the dam follow the road up to the top and enjoy an expansive view over the area.
Then, turn right/north keeping the park to your right following the paved bikeway. Enjoy the view over the park but don't try to cross into it; at the bottom lies impassable marsh land. You reenter the park past the maintenance yard by turning right. Follow the main road of the park until you reach your car again.

The lake at Carbon Canyon Park

▢ Formal Sports Activities

Tennis, Volleyball, Baseball/Softball, Horseshoe Throwing

Tennis: Eight lighted hard courts, good condition.
Volleyball: Three sand volleyball courts and a multi-purpose field.

Tennis courts at Carbon Canyon Park

Baseball/Softball: Two backstops are available for softball games.
Horseshoe Throwing: Horseshoe pits.

Chino Hills State Park

Rating: ●●●●◖
Best Time: Winter, spring or early morning.
Location: 4721 Sapphire Road, Chino Hills. Enter via Carbon Canyon Regional Park. 4442 Carbon Canyon Road, Brea. There are more entrances, but the one through Carbon Canyon can be found easily. (Park headquarters are located in San Bernardino County, 4721 Sapphire Road, Chino Hills.)
Access: From the 55 Freeway going inland take the 91 Freeway going towards Riverside. Exit Imperial Highway, turn left/north. Turn right on Valencia Avenue and right on Carbon Canyon Road. Carbon Canyon Regional Park comes up on your right.

Biking in Chino Hills Park

Profile: A vast area of rolling grassy hills with oaks and sycamores invites mountain bikers and hikers alike to explore. Between 430 feet and the highest elevation of 1,781 feet outdoor athletes can get a good workout on 65 miles of trails.

Facilities: There are no facilities in the Orange County part of Chino Hills Park. Use facilities at Carbon Canyon Park.

For the Hungry and Thirsty: See Carbon Canyon Park.

■ Trail Activities

Hiking, Jogging, Mountain Biking,
Horseback Riding

Trip: Gilman/Sycamore Loop
Mountain Biking, Hiking, Equestrian

Rating: ●●●●●
Distance: Ten miles.
Difficulty: The first part on North Ridge Trail past Gilman Peak is moderate to difficult. The descent on Sycamore Trail poses some moderate to advanced technical difficulties. The return on Telegraph Canyon Trail is mostly easy.
Best Time: Winter, spring or cool days.

Access: Trailhead is at east end of Carbon Canyon Regional Park past the tennis courts. Keep left passing a gate and exit the park following the signs to Chino Hills State Park.

The Trip: After you exit Carbon Canyon Park, go parallel to Carbon Canyon Road for a short distance (0.2 miles) until you reach the signs for Chino Hills State Park to your right. Enter the park and then turn left ascending on North Ridge Trail. The distance from the trailhead to Gilman Peak is four miles of a steady and sometimes steep climb on a fire road accessible to hikers, mountain bikers and equestrians alike. At higher altitudes enjoy expansive views over the coastline, the Pacific Ocean and Catalina Island to the southwest. To the south view the Santa Ana Mountains to the south and to the east/northeast the San Bernardino Mountains.

Pass Gilman Peak, continue to Sycamore Trail and turn right. Follow the single track down watching out for washed out areas and dense vegetation.

At the bottom turn right on Telegraph Canyon Road which is another broad fire road. Telegraph Canyon Road keeps gently going down paralleling and crossing Carbon Canyon Creek several times. You pass through riparian woodland vegetation and can spot wildlife along the way.

This is really one of the more scenic wilderness trails in Orange County. Continue until you reach the exit and return to your car.

A squirrel by the trail

Santa Ana River Trail at Yorba Regional Park

Modification1: Gilman Peak Loop
Hikers and Equestrians only
Rating: ●●●●◖
Distance: Eight miles.
Difficulty: Coming down Gilman Trail can be difficult in part.
Best Time: Winter, spring or morning hours.
The Trip: Everything is the same as in Gilman/Sycamore Loop except the return starts right at Gilman Peak which you climb up. From the peak turn right (west) on Gilman Trail and follow a steep and technically challenging single track down to Telegraph Canyon Road. Even though this trail is designated for hikers and equestrians only, it is used by mountain bikers, so be careful. Turn right at the bottom and proceed as before.
Hikers who want a shorter wilderness experience may prefer this alternative route.

Yorba Regional Park

Rating: ●●●◖ (because of noise background from 91 Freeway).
Best Time: Anytime, since the park offers a lot of shady areas.
Location: 7600 East La Palma, Anaheim, CA.
Access: Take the 55 Freeway to the 91 Freeway going east. Shortly after the two converge, exit at Imperial Highway and turn left/north approximately one-quarter mile. At La Palma, turn right/east and proceed one to one and a half miles to park entry (fee).
Profile: This linear park was once part of a large cattle ranch. The trails of the park connect to the Santa Ana River Trail System leading all the way to the Pacific Ocean in Huntington Beach (22 miles).
Yorba Regional Park provides 175 acres for

The lake at Yorba Regional Park

recreational day use with paved bicycle and rollerblades trails, and unpaved hiking and equestrian trails, which meander through the park, a perfect setting for family excursions.

The equestrian trail runs parallel to the Santa Ana River Trail.

Facilities: Restrooms and drinking fountains, 400 picnic tables, three organized group shelters, and 200 barbecue stoves; playgrounds,

Special Features: Paddle boat and bicycle rentals.

For the Hungry and Thirsty: Concession stands, picnic areas.

■ Trail Activities

Inline Skating, Hiking, Jogging, Biking

Trip 1: Along Yorba Regional Park
Inline Skating, Biking, Jogging, Hiking

Rating: ●●●●

Distance: Five miles round trip.

Difficulty: Easy

Best Time: Cooler season.

Access: Park at the parking lot (free) adjacent to the baseball diamonds and soccer fields at the south end of the park. From there cross over to the Santa Ana River Trail.

The Trip: Once you are on the Santa Ana River Trail, go north along the river. The bike path is in very good shape and it is ideal for inline skating.

There are no inclines or declines. Shortly after you reach the underpass of Weir Canyon Road, return and go back. Pass your starting point and rollerblade to a wooden bridge close to Imperial Highway. Turn around and go back to your starting point.

This is a good trip for families and/or beginners.

Combo: You can connect to the trail system within the park. You can also combine any trail activity with any of the other sports opportunities offered in the park.

Trip 2: The Pond to Yorba Linda
Regional Park (roundtrip) – inline skating

Profile: This trip uses Yorba Regional Park as the turn-around point for a long inline skating trip.

We found it easier to start from the Santa Ana River bikeway near Katella Avenue, as the way back slightly slopes downhill. Of course, you can start at the park, and/or turn around sooner. The trip represents a section of the Santa Ana Bikeway which connects the Santa Ana Mountains to the Pacific Ocean in Huntington Beach.

Rating: ●●●◖ (noise pollution from the freeway).

Best Time: Any time when dry.

Distance: Fourteen miles.

Difficulty: Easy to moderate, but long.

Access: Take Interstate 5 north, turn onto the

California Poppies and Lupines

Santa Ana River Bikeway, Yorba Regional Park

57 Freeway north. Get off at Katella Avenue and turn right. Pass Douglass Road on your left and pull into the parking lot right before the bridge (free parking), across from the Arrowhead Pond of Anaheim.

For the Hungry and Thirsty: Concession stands in Yorba Regional Park, or at the Cafe Perk U Up (adjacent to the parking lot).

The Trip: Park your car and cross the Santa Ana River bridge using the sidewalk of Katella Avenue. After you cross the bridge turn right and right again entering the Santa Ana River Bikeway going towards the mountains which you see in the distance.

In general, the bikeway is in good shape but there are some rough patches. Also watch out if you go in the early morning hours because irrigation overflow will moist the bikeway and make it slippery.

The scenery of the first section to your right (south) will appear industrial. After passing Lincoln Avenue, however, charming backyards, nurseries and several parks characterize the landscape. The last sections before Imperial Highway, the Imperial Woods Trail and Yorba Regional Park, are very scenic.

At Imperial Highway, you have to cross the river in order to get to the Regional Park. We crossed using the paved sidewalk of Imperial Highway rather than the pedestrian bridge. Return the same way.

■ Formal Sports Activities

Volleyball, Baseball, Football, Soccer, Horseshoe Throwing

Volleyball: Several sand volleyball courts .
Baseball: Three lighted ball fields.
Football/Soccer Field
Horse Shoe Pits

Rock Formation in Irvine Regional Park

General Area Orange

→ **Irvine Regional Park**
→ **Santiago Oaks Regional Park**
→ **Peters Canyon Regional Park**

www.cityoforange.com
www.ocparks.com

Orientation:

The City of Orange has historic significance and its Old Town Orange Historic District and Plaza have been repeatedly been voted Orange County's favorite downtown. The circular plaza represents the Mexican influence of the area, and is surrounded by shops and restaurants. The historic district features the second largest concentration of historic buildings in California.

The City of Orange is also home to three outstanding Regional Parks: Irvine Regional Park, Santiago Oaks Regional Park and Peters Canyon Regional Park. They offer abundant trail activities and also opportunities for formal sports.

Among the city parks William O. Hart Memorial Park stands out, providing among other features a swimming pool.

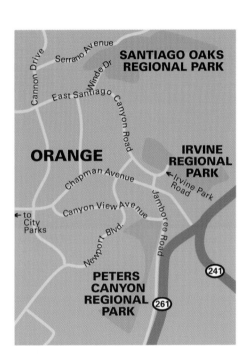

Irvine Regional Park

Rating: ●●●●●
Best time: Year round.
Location: 1 Irvine Park Road, Orange
Access: From 405 or 5 Freeways take Jamboree Road north/east and follow it for eight/five miles until it becomes Irvine Park Road. Turn left into park entrance where you pay.

Irvine Regional Park

Biking in Irvine Regional Park near the entrance

Or take the 55 Freeway to the Chapman Avenue East off ramp. Head east on Chapman for approximately five miles. Turn left on Jamboree Road and find the park entrance after it turns into Irvine Park Road.

Profile: In 1897, James Irvine Jr. donated 160 acres to Orange County making it the first regional park in the area. In later years more land was added. Today, a multitude of recreational opportunities can be found in the 477 acres of the park with its characteristic ancient oak and sycamore groves.

A paved trail runs through the park by which most of its facilities can be reached. Miles of unpaved hiking, mountain biking and equestrian trails surround the park. They provide access to the hillsides offering spectacular views into the park and wilderness areas. Visitors can enjoy eight mostly paved trails or 8.5 miles within the park boundaries.

Native chaparral plants and trees grow in the W. Harding Nature Area and Harding trailhead.

The park is bisected by Santiago Creek (which might be hard to cross after extensive rainfalls). On the hills' lookout points and on the eastside of the creek popular sandstone formations attract visitors.

Two lakes are available for boating and fishing. Abundant opportunities for more formal sports activities are offered.

Facilities: Restrooms, drinking fountains, five

You can rent horses in Irvine Regional Park

W. Harding Nature Area and trailhead

Nature Center in Irvine Regional Park

large group picnic areas, a bandstand/stage, bicycle-, tandem bicycle-, paddle boat rentals.
Special Features: Horse rentals for guided rides on the trails; riding school. For the children pony rides are offered. In addition, the park hosts boarding stables and offers riding lessons.
A nature center explains natural and cultural history.
Another attraction is the Orange County Zoo.
For the Hungry and Thirsty: Many large and small picnic areas. Two snack bars.

■ Trail Activities

Hiking, Running, Mountain Biking, Equestrian, Inline Skating

Trip 1: Horseshoe Loop - Puma Ridge Trail
Hiking

Rating: ●●●●
Distance: Two miles.
Difficulty: Easy to moderate.
Best Time: Cooler season.
Access: The trailhead lies right across the turn into the park entrance. Park inside the park near the entrance and walk back outside. Cross Irvine Park Road and enter the trail.
The Hike: Start your hike going up Horseshoe Loop. After a short distance Puma Trail, a single track, comes up on your right. Turn right and ascend to the ridge. Follow the trail to the

south and enjoy spectacular views. Then descend to Horseshoe Loop and turn left. Pass a lookout point with a cabana on your right; hike back along the old fire road to the starting point. If you take this hike early in the morning, you will probably encounter horseback riders on Horseshoe Loop.

Trip 2: Santiago Oaks Regional Park via Chutes and Goat Mountain - Loop.
Mountain Biking, Hiking

Rating: ●●●●●
Distance: Five miles.
Difficulty: Going up Chutes and down Waterfall is difficult. Going back on Santiago Creek Trail is easy.
Best Time: Cool season.
Access: After you enter the park, you park at parking lot P 3. The trail across from the parking lot is the beginning of Roadrunner Loop.
The Trip: Roadrunner crosses the creek and takes you towards the mountains on a level fire road. To your right, lies Weir Canyon which is open to docent led tours only. Due to the recent land donation by the Irvine Company, it will be gradually opened to the public.
When you come to the far end of Roadrunner you see a gate Weir Canyon 1. You cannot proceed; instead turn left, descend a small hill and find a display board pointing you to the right: Santiago Oaks Regional Park. Follow the

Biking in Santigo Oaks Park

Access: After you enter Irvine Park turn left and park in parking lot P 2. With your bike proceed on the road until you see on your left a sign pointing to Group Area 4. Shortly after, also on your left is the turn off onto the unpaved trails. Enter Santiago Creek Trail going left.

The Ride: Santiago Creek Trail will guide you into Santiago Oaks Regional Park. The trail runs parallel to the Holy Sepulcher Cemetery at a slight elevation. Many more trails, mostly used by equestrians, are on your right closer to the waterway.

After about one and a half miles, close to Villa Park Dam, veer left up the gravel road and right onto a paved road. Shortly after turn left down a steep fire road. Inexperienced riders should walk down. This is the only challenging part of the ride.

At the bottom turn right and cross the creek. You are entering Santiago Oaks Regional Park. Turn left following the trail which is often sandy and thus hard to maneuver. When you cross the creek a second time, you have reached your turn around point. Return the same way.

sign, cross another creek bed which has a steep entry and exit. Then, you will reach a single track trail called The Chutes among mountain bikers. There are no signs.

The Chutes is a favorite downhill for experienced mountain bikers, so be careful at all times. When you come to the top of the trail enjoy the views over the parks and follow the single track ridge line, called Barham Ridge, veering slightly left. This section is quite enjoyable going gently up and down offering always different panoramas over the area.

When you are above the Villa Park Dam, the single track ends in a fire road also called Barham Ridge. Turn left onto the fire road. shortly after, turn right and descend next to mustard plants on Mountain Goat Trail.

On this trail proceed with utmost caution as it is very steep, narrow and has lots of rock outcroppings and wash outs. When you reach the bottom, turn left onto Santiago Creek Trail. Cross the river bed, hike or bike up the steep fire road to your left, turn right onto the paved road, left onto the gravel road; follow Santiago Creek Trail back to Irvine Park for about 1.4 miles.

Trip 3: Irvine Park to Santiago Oaks Park
Mountain Biking, Equestrian, Hiking
Rating: ●●●●
Best Time: Cool season early morning hours.
Distance: 4.5 miles.
Difficulty: Mostly easy, great for families.

■ Formal Sports Activities

Softball/Baseball, Volleyball, Horseshoe Throwing

Baseball/Softball: Four softball fields and several baseball fields.
Volleyball: Several volleyball areas and one sand volleyball court close to the group picnic shelters.
Horseshoe Throwing: Two horseshoe pits.

Santiago Oaks Regional Park

Rating: ●●●●◑
Best time: Any time.
Location: 2145 North Windes Road, Orange.
Access: Coming from the south on 405 Freeway, take the 133 Toll Road north. Merge onto the 241 Toll Road north going toward Riverside. Take the Canyon Road exit toward

Crossing the creek

Chapman Avenue. Turn left on Santiago Canyon Road. Turn right on Jamboree Road. Turn left onto E Santiago Canyon Road. Turn right onto Windes Drive. The park is at the end of Windes. If you come on 55 Freeway in either direction, exit heading east at Katella Avenue/Villa Park, which becomes E.Santiago Canyon Road. Turn left on Windes Drive, which takes you to the park.

Profile: Santiago Oaks Regional Park is a lesser known gem among the Regional Parks. Santiago Creek, which runs through the park, supports a great variety of plant life and wildlife. Ancient live oaks and sycamores populate the canyon. On the north side of the creek visitors can enjoy thousands of planted ornamental trees. The Visitor Center lies adjacent to a five acre Valencia orange grove.

Throughout the park and beyond coyotes, deer, bobcats and, rarely, mountain lions can be seen. In addition, the park is known to be a first class bird watching location for over 130 bird species. The park encompasses 430 acres with a diverse system of thirteen trails for hikers, mountain bikers and horseback riders. To the east the trails connect to the Anaheim Trail system via Peralta Hills Trail and Oak Trail and to the west there is a connection to Irvine Regional Park via Santiago Creek Trail.

Facilities: Restrooms, drinking water, barbecues, playground, a horseshoe pit.

Special Features: Historic Water Dam. The first water dam, built out of clay, was destroyed by floods but rebuilt with rock and cement in 1892. It created one of the first water reservoirs in what was soon to be Orange County.

The Historic Nature Center exhibits the natural and human history of the area with special attention to the wildlife. Park staff offers nature walks and educational programs.

For the Hungry and Thirsty: Enjoy a picnic at the picnic areas. Bring your own provisions.

The water dam in Santiago Oaks Park

■ Trail Activities
Hiking, Mountain Biking, Equestrian

Trip 1: Robber's Peak – Loop
Hiking, Mountain Biking

Rating: ●●●●
Distance: 3.5 miles.
Difficulty: Easy at the bottom of the park, strenuous uphill at the Three B's, and difficult coming down Goat Mountain.
Best Time: Early morning, cooler season.
Access: After you enter the park, turn right and park behind the ranger station. Go back towards the street and cross the creek. Turn right onto Santiago Creek Trail.
The Trip: Santiago Creek Trail is the easy and cool part of the trip because it is level and the many trees protect you from the sun. At Oak Trail take a left turn and start ascending. You will pass two gates. After passing the second you will have left the park and will have entered

the Anaheim Hills Trail. The climb can be strenuous. It culminates at Robber's Peak, a 1,152-foot distinct sandstone peak with lots of history.

On top enjoy sweeping views of the Santa Ana Mountains and the Orange County basin.

Continue on the Anaheim Hills Trail towards the power line tower which is fenced in. To the left of the fence, you will find a sign that just says, "Trail". Follow this trail, which will lead you to the clearly visible ridge trail, Barham Ridge, looping you back towards Santiago Oaks Canyon Park. Don't take the first trail down to the right. Continue on the ridge to the second trail, Mountain Goat Trail, veering off to the right. Before you do that, continue a little further ahead. You will be able to see the water reservoir and Villa Park Dam right below you. Again, enjoy the view, then backtrack to your turn off.

Mountain Goat Trail can be quite narrow, steep and slippery. Make sure to wear hiking boots with traction as you could easily tumble down (For bikers: experts only).

After this challenging descent you will reach Santiago Creek Trail again. Cool off, enjoy the wildlife and return to your starting point.

On top of Robber's Peak

Peters Canyon Regional Park with water reservoir

Equestrian: The Park is very popular among horseback riders, but since there are no public stables, you have to provide your own horse.
Modification: From Santiago Creek Trail bear left onto Historic Dam Trail which extends your trip by 0.4 miles (hikers only).

Peters Canyon Regional Park

Rating: ●●●●
Best Time: Depends on the activity, but in general the cooler season or early morning hours are best, especially nice in early spring.
Location: East Canyon View Avenue, Orange.
Access: From the 405 Freeway exit Jamboree. Take it inland, pass the 5 Freeway and Irvine Boulevard. Turn left on Canyon View Avenue and left again immediately into the parking lot of Peters Canyon Regional Park.
Profile: The Park is relatively small, encompassing 359 acres, but offers a great variety of features serving hikers, mountain bikers and equestrians alike.
One can enjoy over one hundred species of resident and migratory birds in the different areas of the park. It includes Peters Canyon Reservoir with trails leading around it, Peters Canyon Creek with trails along and through it, and East Ridge View Trail offering views over the park and the area.

Extensive and diverse vegetation and wildlife encompass the area. The riparian woodland, the sycamores, willows and cottonwoods sage-scrub and historic eucalyptus groves all provide habitats to the fauna of the park. It includes birds, reptiles and amphibians, bobcats, coyotes, opossums and raccoons.

The trail around the reservoir is well suited for families as it is less than two miles long. A fun trail, especially for children, is the for-hikers-only Peters Canyon Creek Trail offering a natural obstacle course with bridges, water pools and low hanging branches. East Ridge View Trail provides technical difficulties but also great views.

Facilities: Two picnic areas, portable restrooms, water at the parking area, the park office and the information kiosk.
For the Hungry and Thirsty: Bring a snack and have a picnic.

Walking on Big Red Loop in Peters Canyon

■ TRAIL ACTIVITIES:
Hiking, Jogging, Mountain Biking, Equestrian

Trip 1: Peters Canyon Park Reservoir Loop
Hiking, Jogging

Rating: ●●●●
Best Time: Cool season or early mornings, since there is no protection from the sun.
Distance: Two miles.
Difficulty: Easy, with the exception of a steep decline at the west end of the lake.
Access: Trailhead is at the parking lot off East Canyon Avenue.
The Hike: The shortest hike, less than two miles, is pretty and family friendly. From the parking lot head left on the trail starting before the picnic tables to circle the reservoir. At the corner of Canyon View Lane and Jamboree Road turn right following the trail, which turns into a fire road. Keep right and hike up a short, steep incline to reach Peters Canyon Trail.
Take a right again and head down. Again take a right and hike up to the lookout point of the hike, a bench on top of the hill right above the dam. After another right turn you will descend a really steep part of the trail – a challenge for

adults and a delight for children. Now, stay on Lake View Trail following the shoreline of the reservoir. The water and its surrounding vegetation are habitat for a variety of birds such as herons, egrets, grebes, geese and ducks. Lake View Trail will take you back to the parking lot.

Modification: Add Peters Canyon Creek Trail
Hiking , Jogging

Rating: ●●●
Best Time: Cool season or early morning hours.
Distance: 2.5 miles.
Difficulty: Mostly easy.
The Trip: Continue straight on Peters Canyon Trail, a dirt road used by hikers and mountain bikers alike. After about 300 yards south of the dam take Peters Canyon Creek Trail which is only suitable for hikers. This part of the hike is very enjoyable for adults and children as it crosses the creek, winds through thick vegetation, goes through water and, in general, gives a feeling of wilderness. When you come to the end, return the same way, or take Peters Canyon Trail, until you reach the dam where you turn left to resume circling the reservoir.

Trip 2: Peters Canyon Big Red Loop
Mountain Biking, Hiking

Rating: ●●●●
Best Time: Dry and cool season, early morning

Deer observing visitors

Peters Canyon Creek Trail

Distance: Four miles.
Difficulty: First half moderate, second half easy.
Access: Trailhead is at the parking lot off East Canyon Avenue.
The Trip: From the parking lot take Lake View Trail towards Canyon View Avenue which it parallels.
At the intersection of Canyon View and Jamboree Road turn right onto Peters Canyon Trail. In the distance you will see what the local mountain bike riders call Big Red looming. From Peter's Canyon Trail, you'll veer left onto East Ridge View Trail and work your way up the Big Red. Once you are up, you have conquered the hardest part.
Take a break and enjoy the splendid views. From here work your way along the ridge going up and down towards the south end of the park. This part of the trail is steep and narrow; it has many wash-outs and constantly requires your attention. Especially watch out for hikers and other mountain bikers as it can get very busy,

especially on holidays and most weekends.
At the end of the trail turn right onto Eucalyptus Trail and right again on Peters Canyon Trail. Work your way back staying on Peters Canyon Trail which gently ascends, taking you back to Lake View Trail and the parking lot.
For the Hungry and Thirsty: After any excursion to Peters Canyon Regional Park, Irvine Regional Park and Santiago Oaks Regional Park we like to get refreshments at Cyrano's on 7446 East Chapman in Orange. From Peters Canyon Regional Park turn left on Canyon View Avenue, right on Newport Avenue and left into the shopping center parking lot at the corner of Newport and Chapman Avenue. The Cafe is at the north east corner of the center. Cyrano's offers great food, shakes and coffee. It is a hang out for the local mountain bike riders and horse back riders.
Equestrian: The park is popular among horseback riders, no public rides available, provide your own horse.

Campus life at the University of California, Irvine

General Area Irvine

→ **William R. Mason Regional Park**
→ **Orange County Great Park**
→ **City Parks and Other Public Sports Facilities**
→ **Irvine Trails**

www.ci.irvine.ca.com
www.ocparks.com
www.ocgp.org

Orientation:

Development of the City of Irvine started in the 1960s as one of the first mastermind planned communities. Abundant permanently reserved open space was incorporated into the design of a city that hosts one of the leading universities in California.

Irvine is not only consistently rated one of the safest cities in America but also one of the greenest, and most environmentally conscious ones.

The city includes one state park (planning stage), one regional park, over forty city and neighborhood parks and an elaborate trail system going beyond parks and city boundaries. Thus Irvine provides a hard to match abundance of opportunities to the outdoor sport enthusiast. This is why we included many of Irvine's community parks into this activity guide.

The former El Toro Marine Base was recently annexed to the City of Irvine to form the Orange County Great Park which will provide a wide variety of active and passive uses, miles of walking and biking trails, and Orange County's largest sports park.

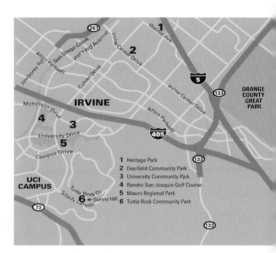

1 Heritage Park
2 Deerfield Community Park
3 University Community Park
4 Rancho San Joaquin Golf Course
5 Mason Regional Park
6 Turtle Rock Community Park

Hiking in Shady Canyon, Irvine

Inline skating in Mason Park, Irvine

William R. Mason Regional Park

Rating: ●●●●◖
Best time: Year round.
Location: 18712 University Drive, Irvine CA
Access: From the 405 Freeway exit Culver Drive. Go south on Culver Drive, turn right on University Drive. Turn left into park entrance (fee). Free for bikers and hikers.
Profile: William Mason Regional Park, (349 acres), consists of two independent parts. The section between Harvard Drive and Culver Drive (A) is developed and features large grassy areas, two sand volleyball courts, a fitness course, a paved trail system, and a nine acre lake. It is an ideal place for group activities.
The second part (B), 123 acre, extends north from Culver Drive up to Ridgeline Drive and features a botanical preserve with wildlife and rare and endangered bird species, like the California Gnatcatcher.
The main paved walkway bisects the park lengthwise with several trails branching off to the left and right. The trails are ideal for inline skating, biking and walking and connect to the larger Irvine bicycle trail system.
Facilities: Restrooms, picnic shelters, playgrounds, amphitheater.
For the Hungry and Thirsty: Bring your own provisions and enjoy them in one of the many picnic shelters (Part A only).

■ Trail Activities
Walking, Jogging, Biking, Inline Skating

Trip: Through Mason Park
Inline Skating, Jogging

Rating: ●●●◖
Distance: Two miles.
Difficulty: Easy
Best Time: Any, except holiday weekends.
Access: After entering the park at the main entrance at University Drive turn right after you pay your entrance fee at the ranger station. Go as far as possible and park in parking area P1.
The Trip: One of the trails mostly follows the park boundaries. From parking area P1 find the trail that circles the park and follow it to the left. Cross the drainage channel and turn left. At this

Soccer game in Mason Park, Irvine

A jogger surrounds the lake in Mason Park

The lake at Mason Regional Park in Irvine

juncture the trail goes through hilly terrain. Pass the amphitheatre. At the next intersection keep going straight and cross the drainage channel a second time. After rains, this crossing is closed. Take an alternate slightly shorter route not crossing the channel initially but going along the lake. The two trails join after the second drainage channel crossing.

Keep the lake on your left, pass a large ball field with several stations of a fitness par course. Keep to the right of the field and continue on the trail. After you pass the restroom building turn right.Turn left shortly before you reach the parking area P7 close to an exit to Culver Drive. You will pass a picnic shelter and a playground. At the parking area P4 the trail veers off to the left. Cross the grass and enter the trail running parallel to the creek and University Drive. Turn left. Follow the trail, pass the main entrance, and arrive at the second exit to University Drive where you turn left. Find your car again at P1.

Modification: You can combine part A and B of William Mason Park.

Distance: Four miles.

The Trip: When you come to the section close to P4 while circling the park, after you cross the grassy section turn right on the trail that parallels the creek and University Drive. The trail exits the park at the corner of University Drive and Culver Drive.

Cross Culver Drive and turn right. After 100 yards you will find the entrance to part B of William Mason Park. Continue on the main trail passing through a nature reserve and return when you reach Jeffrey Road. Retrace your steps and reenter William Mason Park on the other side of Culver Drive; continue as described above.

▮ Formal Sports Activities
Volleyball, Ball Games, Horseshoe Throwing

Volleyball: Two sand volleyball courts.
Ball Field: One large mult-iuse ball field.
Horse Shoe Throwing: One horse shoe pit.

Orange County Great Park

Orange County Great Park
(planning stage)

Rating: ●●●●●
Best time: Any time.
Location: The street address of the future headquarters is not available at this point. The Balloon and Visitor Center within the Great Park are accessible by W Marine Way, Irvine. The Park lies geographically in the center of Orange County. 133 and the 241 Toll roads, Barranca Parkway and Alton Parkway border the Great Park; it is bisected by Irvine Boulevard.
Access: Access to the Balloon and Visitor Center: From the 405 Freeway exit Sand Canyon and head north. Turn right on Marine Way, left on Perimeter Way. Follow the signs to the Balloon. Parking is to the right.
Profile: Roughly twice the size of New York's Central Park, the Orange County Great Park encompasses 1,300 acres. Award-winning design features the latest environmental innovations focusing on sustainability and conservation of energy. A three mile long

Wildlife Corridor will link Cleveland National Forest on Orange County's western border to Crystal Cove State Park and the Pacific Ocean. A Great Canyon (60 feet deep) will invite the visitor to stroll on trails through native vegetation and along a creek crossed by several bridges.
Furthermore Botanical Gardens and a Cultural Terrace will be featured as will a 165-acre sports park for more formal sports activities like soccer, baseball, skateboarding, and rock climbing. A great lawn will be available for all kinds of outdoor activities and field play within the sports park section.
The bicycle trails of the Great Park will connect to the Irvine trail system. The hiking trails will vary from easy to challenging.
Facilities: Restrooms, picnic lawn.
Special Features: A Great Park Balloon invites visitors to tethered balloon rides up to 500 feet high offering beautiful panoramas over Orange County.
A visitor center showcases design of the park and offers amenities. The center is located in the 27-acre preview park which is open to the public. The preview park also includes a WWII aircraft hangar, a promenade with seating areas, a plaza and a large picnic lawn which all can be rented out for events.
For the Hungry and Thirsty: At this time vending machines. In the future the cultural terrace will be the site for restaurants and cafes.

Irvine City Parks and other Public Sports Facilities

Colonel Bill Barber Marine Corps Memorial Park
Rating: ●●●●◖
Best time: Year round.
Location: 4 Civic Center Plaza, between Alton and Barranca Parkways off Harvard.
Access: From the 405 Freeway exit at Culver Drive. Go inland and turn left on Alton Parkway. Turn right on Harvard and left into the

parking lot of the Civic Center and the park.

Profile: Bill Barber Park, adjacent to the Civic Center of Irvine, boasts many features for the more formal sports enthusiast. Soccer, baseball and tennis players find state of the art facilities. In addition, the park has access to the Irvine bicycle trail system.

One can also walk or run the perimeter of the 42-acre park. There is access to the Irvine trail system.

Facilities: Restrooms, drinking fountains, picnic shelters, barbecues, playgrounds.

For the Hungry and Thirsty: Concession stands.

▪ Formal Sports Activities

Tennis, Softball, Soccer, Baseball

Tennis: The park is especially noteworthy for its six lighted tennis courts in excellent shape.

Softball: Three lighted softball diamonds.

Soccer: Three lighted fields.

Baseball: Stadium, batting cages.

Heritage Park

Rating: ●●●●●

Best time: Any

Location: 14301 Yale Avenue at the corner of Walnut and Yale.

Access: Going south on Interstate 5   exit Jeffrey Avenue. Stay in the straight lane; it will become Walnut Street after you cross Jeffrey Avenue. Going north, exit Jeffrey Avenue and turn left, then right on Walnut Street. Proceed to Yale Avenue, turn right and left into the parking lot.

Profile: Heritage Park is the jewel among Irvine community parks. It offers great opportunities for more formal sport activities.

Qualifying swim competitions for the 1984 Olympics were held at the Heritage Park Aquatics Center. The complex was upgraded and renamed as the Woollett Aquatics Center.

Facilities: Restrooms, drinking fountains, great playgrounds, one amphitheater, two concession stands, barbecues, one group picnic area, picnic tables and electrical outlets.

Heritage Park, Irvine

Tennis courts in Heritage Park, Irvine

Other Attractions: The Heritage Park Regional Library and the Irvine Fine Arts Center are also part of the park.
For the Hungry and Thirsty: Concession stands.

▓ Formal Sports Activities
Swimming, Tennis, Basketball, Baseball, Racquetball, Soccer, Volleyball.

Swimming: The outstanding complex features two Olympic size pools for swimming competition, and a large teaching pool.
Tennis: Many community, competitive or instructional tennis activities take place on the eight lighted tennis courts at Heritage Park, but they are also available for walk-on tennis.
Basketball: Three lighted basketball courts.
Baseball: Two lighted ball diamonds.
Racquetball: Two lighted racquetball courts.
Soccer: Three lighted soccer fields.
Volleyball: One volleyball court.

University Community Park
Rating: ●●●●
Best time: Any
Location: 1 Beech Tree Lane, Irvine.
Access: From the 405 Freeway exit Culver Drive and go south. Turn left on Michelson Drive, right on Sandburg Way, left on Lexicon Street into the park.
Profile: University Community Park offers

One of the three pools at Heritage Park

many amenities. The sports facilities are geared more towards the formal sports enthusiast. The park can be reached easily by bike, because it is in the vicinity of the Irvine trail system.

Facilities: Restroom, drinking fountains, playgrounds, group picnic area.

Special Features: Irvine's Adventure Playground is located at the park.

Other Attractions: Located adjacent to the park is the University Park Library with a collection of over 95,000 books

Formal Sports Activities
Frisbee-Golf, Basketball, Volleyball, Soccer, Baseball

Frisbee-Golf: The golf like game, where the player has to hit targets with flying discs, is getting more and more popular. The nine-hole course at University Community Park includes two pole hole baskets.

Tennis: Four lighted tennis courts.
Basketball: One court
Volleyball: Two lighted courts.
Soccer: Two lighted soccer fields.
Baseball: One lighted diamond.

Deerfield Community Park:
Rating: ●●●●
Best Time: Any
Location: 55 Deerwood West, Irvine
Access: From the 405 Freeway exit Culver

Disc golf at Deerfield Park, Irvine

Grassy area at Turtle Rock Park, Irvine

Drive, go inland. Turn right on Irvine Center Drive and left on Deerwood

Profile: Deerfield Community Park is small but well kept. It offers a variety of athletic amenities. It can be accessed through the Irvine trail system.

Facilities: Restrooms, drinking fountains, playgrounds barbecues, one group picnic area, picnic tables and electrical outlets.

For the Hungry and Thirsty: Concession stands.

Formal Sports Activities
Frisbee-Golf, Tennis, Volleyball, Racqetball

Frisbee-Golf: The course at Deerfield Community Park offers a good variey of targets.
Tennis: Four lighted tennis courts.
Volleyball: Two lighted volleyball courts.
Racquetball: Two racquetball courts.

Turtle Rock Community Park
Rating: ●●●●◖
Best Time: All year.
Location: 1 Sunny Hill Drive, Irvine.
Access: From expressway 405 exit University Drive; turn left on Ridgeline, left again on Turtle Rock Drive, another left turn on Sunnyhill Drive; turn right into the parking lot.
Profile: This small park is a jewel due to its serene location and its very well landscaped grounds. It also serves as a trailhead going into

Harvard Skating Park, Irvine

The tennis courts at Turtle Rock Park

Shady Canyon or surrounding wilderness areas.
Special Features: Turtle Rock Nature Center.
Facilities: Drinking fountains, restrooms, playground, picnic tables, barbecues.
For the Hungry and Thirsty: Bring a picnic.

▓ Formal Sports Activities
Volleyball, Tennis, Basketball, Baseball,

Volleyball: Two sand volleyball courts.
Tennis: Four tennis courts in great shape.
Basketball: One half court.
Baseball: Lighted ball diamond.
Large multi-purpose grassy area.

Harvard Skate Park
Rating: ●●●●
Best Time: All year.
Location: Adjacent to Harvard Athletic Park at

14701 Harvard Avenue between Irvine Center Drive and Walnut Street.
Access: From 405 Freeway exit Jamboree Road, go inland. Turn right on Walnut Street and right on Harvard Avenue. The Park is on your right.
Profile: Harvard Athletic Park offers many opportunities for most sports.
The skateboard park, on the southwest end of Harvard Park provides features like Pyramid, Spine, Bowl, and Rails. Protective gear must be worn (to be rented at the entrance).
Facilities: At Harvard Athletic Park.

Rancho San Joaquin Golf Course
Rating: ●●●●
Best Time: Any
Location: I Ethel Coplen Way, Irvine.
Access: From 405 Freeway exit Culver Drive and go south. Turn right on Ethel Coplen Way. Go to the end of street and into the parking lot.
Profile: One of the better public eighteen hole courses in Orange County.
It offers 65 lighted stalls, separate chipping and approach areas, bunkers for practice.

Irvine Area Trails
Hiking, Jogging, Biking, Inline Skating

Profile: Irvine is one of the best places in Orange County for trail activities, especially biking. Abundant well landscaped trails

A game of volleyball at Turtle Rock Park

Hiking and biking in Irvine

meander through the city and its parks and connect to trails beyond city borders.

Trip 1: Strawberry Fields Loop
Inline Skating

Rating: ●●●◖
Distance: Six miles.
Difficulty: Easy to moderate.
Best Time: Any
Access: William Mason Park, see p. 170.
For the Hungry and Thirsty: At Tannaka Farms we like to pick strawberries during the season. Eateries at Woodbridge Village Center.
The Trip: Start south at William Mason Park along Sand Canyon Wash until you reach Culver Drive. Cross Culver, enter the park's wilderness section 100 yards down. Follow the bikeway through the park to the other end at Ridgeline Drive, which you cross.

Follow the bikeway leaving Tannaka Farms and Strawberry Farms to your right. You are paralleling University Drive until you reach 405 Freeway, where the bikeway veers to the right; cross the bridge. Turn left and then right on Jeffrey Drive. Pass Alton Parkway, San Diego

Creek Channel and turn sharp right at the beginning of the bikeway which parallels the channel. You pass Jeffrey through a tunnel. Beware: poor visibility, rough surface.

Shortly after you cross Creek Road, Woodbridge Village Center comes up to your right. Turn left taking the pedestrian bridge crossing the channel. Pass through Woodbridge Community Park, and cross another pedestrian bridge over Alton Parkway. You can see South Lake Park coming up to the right.

Keep following the bikeway which veers to the left after the bridge; then turn right paralleling Springbrook South. After you pass the tennis courts at South Lake Park the bikeway turns away from Springbrook. Following it you cross Yale Loop entering Yale Avenue.

Another pedestrian bridge will take you over the 405 Freeway. Stay on Yale Avenue, cross Michelson Drive and University Drive; reenter Mason Park. Return to where you parked.

Modification: Instead of turning left across from Woodbridge Village, go straight following the bikeway along San Diego Creek Channel. This section extends your skating experience by five miles. For directions see p. 178.

Irvine Loop Trail, section along San Diego Creek Channel

Trip 2: Strictly Irvine Loop
Biking, Inline Skating

Rating: ●●●●
Distance: Twelve miles roundtrip.
Difficulty: Easy
Best Time: Any time, but not after heavy rains.
Access: It is best to start from Irvine Civic Center/Colonel Barber Park, since it provides free parking. See ppxxx. Park close to the river.
The Ride: Find access to the bicycle trail, paralleling the river. Go towards the mountains. Soon the trail will take a right turn. After one third of a mile you reach Harvard Avenue.
Leave the bike trail, cross Harvard Avenue and Barranca Parkway and enter the trail running along Harvard Avenue. This is the least pleasant part of the ride, since you are close to the street and you have to cross at traffic lights.
Once you get to Deerfield Avenue, cross the train tracks and Harvard Avenue and enter the trail that runs along the train tracks to the left.
After a quarter of a mile the trail takes a sharp turn and then follows the river.
Soon, you will find yourself next to a long concrete river channel passing under Interstate 5 (this route works only at low water levels).
Soon after, the bikeway veers away from the channel and runs along 261 tollroad at a distance. By reaching Portola Parkway, you are at the end of the Irvine bike trail.
Return the same way until you reach Deerfield Avenue. Cross the train tracks and Harvard Avenue again and enter the bike trail, which runs along the train tracks starting at a vegetable field.
You stay on this trail until you reach Sand Canyon Avenue. There, head south, pass Barranca Parkway, the river and enter the bike trail on the south side of the river.
At Culver Drive turn right, soon after find the sharp right turn that will take you to the underpass at Culver Drive. Now, stay on the bikeway paralleling the river, until your starting point comes up on your left.
This ride is very enjoyable and shows many pretty sights of Irvine.

Modification: Irvine to Ocean (Roundtrip)
Rating: ●●●●◖
Distance: Roundtrip thirty miles (XXL).
Difficulty: Easy to moderate.
For the Hungry and Thirsty: See Newport Beach: Balboa Peninsula and Back Bay.
The Trip: Continue on the bikeway along the channel towards the ocean, passing under 405 Freeway, 73 Toll Road and Jamboree Road,

whereafter you reach Upper Back Bay.

There the bikeway takes a sharp left turn and you ride along the Bay parallel to Jamboree Road. Take a right turn at Eastbluff Drive, and go slightly uphill.

Stop on top at the viewpoint overlooking Back Bay, before you take a steep downhill on Back Bay Drive, which is one way for cars in the opposite direction. Beware, and stay to the right on the bike trail. Riding along Back Bay for about three miles is the best part of the ride.

Close to its end Back Bay Drive takes a sharp left turn. There, on the left side of the entrance to the parking lot to the Dunes take the pedestrian trail up to Bayview Park on top (another great view over Back Bay). Keep to the left and cross Pacific Coast Highway. Bike downhill and enter Balboa Island on Marine Avenue after you cross the bridge.

Take the first right on North Bayfront and follow it to Agate Avenue, where you take a left turn. That leads you to the Balboa Island

Ferry. Take the nostalgic ferry to Balboa Peninsula. Follow Palm Street straight to the beach near Balboa Pier, enjoy the vista and a swim.

For more information on Back Bay, Balboa Island and the Peninsula, see the chapter on Newport Beach.

Trip 3: From Irvine towards the Mountains
Biking

Rating: ●●●◖

Distance: Fourteen miles roundtrip.

The Ride: Start as in trip 2. After you reach the concrete river channel watch out for Bryant Avenue.

Leave Peter's Canyon Trail and cross the 261 Toll Road on Bryant Avenue. After crossing turn right following the bikeway which meanders through residential areas. You will pass by the original Irvine Ranch on your left. You can take a little detour to visit the Ranch by taking a left

Top of the hill, Back Bay Drive. Irvine to Ocean trip

on Jamboree Road, a left on Irvine Boulevard and then another left on Old Myford Road.

If you skip the detour, follow the bikeway which parallels Jamboree Road towards the mountains. After passing Trevino Drive, enter Valencia Park.

At the end of the park the trail leads to the other side of Jamboree Road by an underpass. It keeps following Jamboree Road, then Portola Parkway to the left, Tustin Ranch Road to the right and Pioneer Road to the left. Here the trail leaves the road and goes along Cedar Grove Park, a small park with a beautiful Cedar Grove.

You pass a school on your right and then ride parallel Peters Canyon Road until you reach the south end of Peters Canyon Regional Park. On a mountain bike it is fun to enter the park and try out some trail. See the Orange chapter.

On street bike turn around and retrace your trip.

Trip 4: Woodbridge Loop
Biking (Loop). Walking and Jogging
(Shady Canyon Trail, Quail Hills Trail)

Rating: ●●●●◖
Distance: Sixteen miles.
Difficulty: Easy to strenuous.
Best Time: Cooler season, early morning hours
Access: For access and parking see directions to Turtle Rock Community Park (p. 175).
For the Hungry and Thirsty: On your way: Lucca Cafe at 6507 Quail Hill Parkway, Irvine. When you come down from Shady Canyon Trail on Shady Canyon Avenue, turn right on Quail Hill Parkway amd cross over to enter health oriented Lucca Cafe tucked to your right in the Quail Hill Shopping Center. Also, Mimi's Cafe at 4030 Barrance Parkway, Irvine. Before the underpass of Culver Drive, turn right into a parking lot; the cafe is at your left.
The Trip: Head into Shady Canyon Community where Shady Canyon Drive and Sunnyhill intersect. Leave the guard house to your right and follow the foot path into the gated community. The trail ascends and leads to the

other entrance to Shady Canyon Community. Enjoy the view to your left over the great scenery including Strawberry Hill Golf Course. Follow the trail all the way up and then descend on Shady Canyon Drive. At the bottom, cross over 405 Freeway, then cross Alton Way to Sand Canyon. Continue straight on the left/north side of Sand Canyon on the bicycle trail until you reach San Diego Creek Channel shortly before Barranca Parkway.

Turn left on the bike trail running along the creek on its left/west side. Depending upon the season you might spot rare birds in the creek bed; for it is a bird sanctuary during dry season. Follow the trail until you reach Jeffrey Road, then turn right. After you cross the creek, continue for about one hundred yards. The bike trail starts again with a sharp right turn taking you through a tunnel under Jeffrey Road.

Now you ride along San Diego Creek Channel on an uninterrupted stretch of bike trail for quite a while. You pass under Yale Loop, Creek Road, Lake Road and Culver Drive (Mimi's Cafe).

When you continue your trip you pass Harvard Avenue, you cross the creek at Colonel Barber Memorial Park, and you pass Irvine Civic Center on the left. Furthermore you pass Alton Parkway, Main Street, 405 Freeway, Michelson

Quail Hills Trail (dry season)

Active in Shady Canyon

Street, and finally Rancho San Joaquin Golf Course. At the end of the golf course runs University Drive.

Leave the trail turning left, cross University Drive and Harvard Avenue and enter William Mason Park on your right. Follow the bike trail through the park, paralleling University Drive. You leave the park at the corner of University Drive and Culver Drive, where you cross and turn right.

After about fifty yards turn left into Mason Park. Leave University High to your right and turn right at the second intersection, exiting the park. Follow the trail veering to the right on Cobblestone Street, and left on Campus Drive. Pass under Turtle Rock Drive and follow the trail until it ends at the corner of Turtle Rock Drive and Starcrest.

There you can choose: either you go straight on Turtle Rock Drive for an easier ride or go right on Starcrest for a final strenuous climb. In case you choose the easier route stay on Turtle Rock Drive and cross Ridgeline. Turn left on Sunnyhill Drive and ride directly into the parking lot of Turtle Rock Community Park.

If you prefer the more difficult route on Starcrest, turn right on Ridgeline, then right on Turtle Rock Drive, left on Sunnyhill, where a right turn takes you to the parking lot of Turtle Rock Park.

This pleasant trip mostly follows bike trails and lasts about an hour and a half without a break.

Modification: After you descend on Shady Canyon Drive, you can extend your bike ride by almost two miles, if you take the beautiful Quail Hills Trail. This is an off road biking experience, where the urban development disappears at various places.

Taking Quaill Hills Trail makes a scenic trip for walking or jogging.

Santa Ana Mountains

General Area Santa Ana Mountains And Southern Foothills

→ **Limestone Canyon and Whiting Ranch Wilderness Park**
→ **O'Neill Regional Park**
→ **Thomas F. Riley Wilderness Park**
→ **Santa Ana Mountain Trails**

www.ocparks.com
www.irvineranchconservancy.org

Equestrians in the Santa Ana Mountains

Orientation:

The Santa Ana Mountains and their southern foothills make great scenery for the outdoor person who likes to exercise in wilderness areas. In 2010, OC parkland was increased by 20.000 acres through a protected open space donation by the Irvine Company.

Within the neighborhood of Lake Forest, Trabuco Canyon, Rancho Santa Margerita, and Coto de Caza you can explore three great parks in the foothills:

Limestone Canyon and Whiting Ranch Wilderness Park is the most northern of the three. The Limestone canyon section is presently accesisible on a limited basis. It will gradually open to the public.The Whiting Ranch Section is rather small, but its diversity highlighted by scenic rock formations, is well worth a visit, even though it is still recovering from the 2007 Santiago fire.

Located in Trabuco Canyon, O'Neill Regional Park stretches for ten miles from a mountainous northern wilderness along a valley area including campgrounds to its southwestern part, where the Arroyo Trabuco area was recently added to the park. You will mostly find equestrians and hikers here.

Thomas F. Riley Wilderness Park neighboring the community of Coto de Caza is a wildlife sanctuary of rolling hills, canyons and grassland, used by hikers, mountain bikers, and equestrians.

The Santa Ana Mountains extend for about thirty-five miles from the northeast to the southeast county line of Orange and Riverside Counties.

Santiago Peak with its 5687 feet is the highest mountain in the area.The Sant Ana Mountains host a great variety of flora and fauna. Large wilderness areas have fortuately been protected from threats of expanding transportation and urban development.

A multitude of trails crisscross the mountain range offering many opportunities for activities. The trips suggested in the following are just a few attractive samples of outdoor exercising in the Santa Ana Mountains.

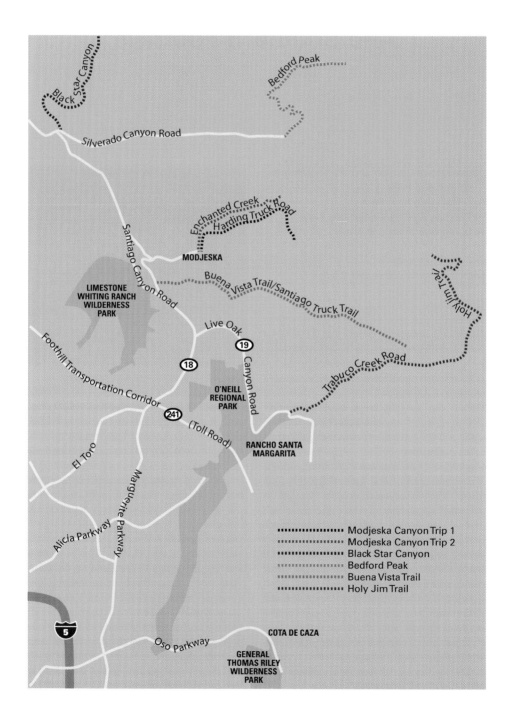

Star Canyon

Black

Bedford Peak

Silverado Canyon Road

Enchanted Creek
Harding Truck Road

MODJESKA

Santiago Canyon Road

LIMESTONE
WHITING RANCH
WILDERNESS
PARK

Buena Vista Trail/Santiago Truck Trail

Holy Jim Trail

Live Oak

19

18

Canyon Road

Foothill Transportation Corridor

Trabuco Creek Road

O'NEILL
REGIONAL
PARK

241

(Toll Road)

RANCHO SANTA
MARGARITA

El Toro

Marguerite Parkway

Alicia Parkway

•••••••••••••••• Modjeska Canyon Trip 1
•••••••••••••••• Modjeska Canyon Trip 2
•••••••••••••••• Black Star Canyon
•••••••••••••••• Bedford Peak
•••••••••••••••• Buena Vista Trail
•••••••••••••••• Holy Jim Trail

5

COTA DE CAZA

Oso Parkway

GENERAL
THOMAS RILEY
WILDERNESS
PARK

Hiking Whiting Ranch Wilderness Park

Limestone Canyon and Whiting Ranch Wilderness Park

Rating: ●●●●◖

Best time: Year round. Check for park opening after rain.

Location/Access: The park has two entry points: To reach the park from Interstate 5, take the Bake exit, turn left (east), proceed to Portola Parkway (about 5 miles), turn left on Portola Parkway, then continue one half mile to Market; turn right. Market Place parking lot and the park entrance are to your immediate left (fee).

To reach the Glenn Ranch Road entrance, turn right on Portola Parkway, left on Glenn Ranch Road, left into parking lot.

An additional 87-acre parcel adjacent to El Toro Road and the Aliso Creek Bike Path, known as the McFadden Ranch House, includes the Ranger Station and Interpretive Center.

Profile: Whiting Ranch Wilderness Park encompasses 1.500 acres.

Its main entrance lies adjacent to a shopping center. One would not expect a wilderness preserve nestled between sprawling suburbia, but half a mile into the park, one can see mule deer and other wildlife enjoy seasonal streams, majestic oaks, sycamores and other types of vegetation.

The most picturesque spot is Red Rock Canyon, open to hikers only. Great vistas can be enjoyed from Four Corners and other lookout points.

The park was once part of the original ranches of Orange County. In 1988 the area was dedicated to be an open space wilderness park. The park offers fifteen miles of trails for bikers, horseback riders and hikers. Some trails are for hikers only. For bikers the recommended course is clockwise around the park to avoid collisions with other bikers and hikers.

Facilities: Porta-potties close to main entrance.

Special Features: Red Rock Canyon. Red Rock Canyon is surrounded by striking 100-foot eroded sandstone cliffs. The rock formations contain marine fossils from about twenty

Red Rock Canyon in Whiting Ranch Park

million years ago. To preserve the fragile environment it is open to hikers only.

For the Hungry and Thirsty: Cafes and restaurants in shopping center next to main entrance.

■ Trail Activities

Hiking, Jogging, Mountain Biking

Trip: Borrego Trail – Four Corners Loop
Mountain Biking

Distance: 5.5 miles (about 1.15 hours).

Difficulty: Intermediate with some easy parts aand a few strenuous inclines.

Best Time: Dry season since Borrego Trail can get submerged after rainfalls. Morning hours are best for exposed trails and for wildlife viewings.

Access: Start from the main entrance to the park on Marketplace.

The Ride: The entrance to the park and the first half of Borrego Trail feel choked from suburban development on the sides.

Soon, though, development ceases and one leaves civilization.

behind. The trail provides moderate challenges. going through water and over rocky and sandy terrain. Most of Borrego Trail is shaded by oak trees and sycamores running along a creek.

The incline starts at Mustard Road. Turn right and start your climb. This part of the trip can be quite strenuous, since the trees retreat as you go up, and the sun beats down.

Up at Four Corners, take a rest and enjoy the exhilarating view over Whiting Ranch Wilderness Park and Santiago Canyon.

Hiking can be strenuous, hiking poles help

Continue with another short climb taking Whiting Road which starts descending shortly after, forking off into Serrano Road and Line Shack Trail. Stay on Serrano Road which brings you back to the cool and shaded area of the park. In this area you may surprise deer grazing, during the quiet morning hours.

Exit the park on Portola Parkway, turn right and follow Portola for a mile until you reach a nice little café at the shopping center.

Modification: Mountain biking Borrego Trail and part Mustard Road, hiking Red Rock Trail.

Distance: 1.5 miles biking to trailhead, 1.5 miles hiking. Then four more miles biking.

Difficulty: Easy to strenuous.

Best Time: Not during wet season since the bike trail gets submerged at places; not when it is hot since the hiking trail is exposed to the sun.

The Trip: This park offers a fabulous combination of mountain biking and hiking. You start the same way as with the previous ride taking Borrego Trail to Mustard Road turning right. After a short distance take a left turn at Red Rock Trail, and leave your bikes and lock them to a tree. This trail is for hikers only. You hike up Red Rock Trail which can be a bit steep and narrow towards the end.

You'll be rewarded with red eroded sand stone cliffs that were formed about twenty million years ago of ocean sediments. The cliffs contain fossilized marine life.

This is a magic place where you can meditate with nature. We went on a brisk and sunny winter morning and did not encounter another soul. Head back the same way, fetch your bikes and continue on Mustard Road as in Borrego Trail – Four Corners Loop.

Special Features: Red Rock Canyon, picturesque ancient sand stone cliffs.

■ Trail Activities
Walking/Hiking, Jogging/Running

Billy Goat Trail
Hiking
Rating: ●●● to ●●●●
Distance: Five miles.
Difficulty: Moderate to strenuous.
Best Time: Cool season, early morning hours. Billy Goat Trail is exposed to the sun.
Access: Start from the main entrance to the park at Marketplace.
The Hike: From the parking lot take shady Borrego Trail until you reach Mustard Road. Turn right and shortly after turn left on Red Rock Canyon Trail.

About a quarter of a mile into Red Rock Canyon, Billy Goat Trail turns off to the right. It winds through prime Coastal Sage Scrub habitat, up rocky ridges and through scenic canyons. The narrow trail provides a great experience with the coastal sage habitat and its wildlife. Extreme up and down elevations create

A picnic area in O'Neill Park

a challenge. At Spur Road turn right and proceed to Four Corners with its great panorama and turn right going down on Mustard Road. Return the same way you came.

O'Neill Regional Park

Rating: ●●●●
Best time: Year round.
Location: 30892 Trabuco Canyon Road, Trabuco Canyon,
Access: From Interstate 405 take the 133 Toll Road north, the 241 Toll Road south towards Rancho Santa Margarita. Exit Santa Margarita turn left, left again on Plano Trabuco. Plano Trabuco becomes Trabuco Canyon Road. Park entrance comes up on your left.
Or take 405 or I 5 south, exit El Toro, turn left towards the mountains and follow it all the way until you reach Trabuco Canyon Road, turn right. Park entrance comes up on your right.
Profile: O'Neill Park consists of three different parts. After you enter, to the right hand side lies mountainous wilderness with miles of trails for hiking, mountain biking and equestrian use. Its peak, Vista Point, offers one of the best views of Orange County with vistas all the way to the ocean on clear days.
Located straight ahead in the valley and to the left on a terrace overlooking the park are day

use sites and campsites, including an equestrian campsite as well as playgrounds and a nature center.
The third area extends for miles from the southwestern end of the park with the Arroyo Trabuco Trail connecting to the Tijeras Creek Trail. This area is basically comprised of the two riverbeds and trails crisscrossing through them.
You will find hikers and mountain bikers here, but the park is particularly well suited for equestrian use as the many adjacent stables can attest to.
Facilities: Campgrounds, group campsites, equestrian campground, restrooms, showers, nature center, playground, picnic shelters, water fountains.
Special Features: The Nature Center with exhibits pertaining to the natural and cultural history of the Santa Ana Mountains. Also guided nature tours are provided upon reservation.
For the Hungry and Thirsty: Inside the park, bring your own supplies and enjoy at the many fire rings, BBQs and picnic shelters.
Outside the park, you can try out Cook's Corner on 19152 Trabuco Canyon Road a few minutes away from O'Neill Park. It offers juicy burgers and fries along with lots of peanuts. On Sundays you can see hundreds of motor bikers. Sometimes you can listen to live music. It's raunchy!

Garland Daisies

Mountain biking on Arroyo Trabuco Trail

■ Trail Activities

Hiking, Mountain Biking, Equestrian.

Trip 1: Arroyo Trabuco Trail
Mountain Biking

Rating: ●●●
Distance: Six miles one way.
Difficulty: Easy
Best Time: Dry but cool season.
Access: Find the trailhead off the main park road towards the south end of the park. A sign guides you to the Arroyo Trabuco trailhead where you pass through a gate.
Other Attractions: The campsite of the Portola Expedition in July 1769 at the fork of Arroyo Trabuco Trail and Loop Trail. The expedition was looking for suitable locations for missions.
The Trip: Follow the trail that meanders along the Trabuco Creek, crossing it several times and also crossing several side arms of it. Depending on the time of the year you might get wet.

At the beginning of the trail you pass first under a massive bridge, the Foothill Transportation Corridor Toll Road. A bit further ahead you pass under another massive construction, Santa Margarita Parkway. Let that not disenchant you. 2000 trees were planted along the creek in exchange for the damage done by construction of the toll road.

About two miles into the ride, after the first Trabuco Creek crossing, the trail gently ascends to another access point to the trail off Arroyo Vista which offers plenty of parking.

The trail continues sloping to the right. You will reach a Y-fork of Loop Trail which curves off to the right and Trabuco Trail going straight staying on the mesa. At the fork you'll find a historic plaque marking the campsite of the Portola expedition in 1769.

After that, you'll descend back to the canyon bottom. These last two miles of the ride are the most attractive ones as you bike through grassy clearings dotted with ancient oaks and

Equestrians like O'Neill Park

The Trip: Live Oak Trail takes you to the northwest Rim of the Park. It starts elevating gently. You will encounter a fork where you turn right. You reach a paved road leading to a water tower, where you turn left. After about 200 yards Live Oak Trail continues to the left and guides you up to the rim.

Up here the trail is mostly level with some short steep inclines and declines. If you want to avoid the last and longest steep incline take Coyote Trail which veers off to the right; otherwise continue on Live Oak Trail until you reach the peak where it intersects with Vista Trail.

Enjoy one of the most stunning views of all hikes sweeping from Saddleback Mountain over to the Pacific Ocean.

After taking a break continue on Vista Trail which provides more beautiful views and gently takes you down to Hoffman Homestead Trail on which you turn right. Down in the canyon you can cool off under large sycamore oaks and other trees. This very pleasant section of the trail takes you back to the park entrance sloping parallel to Trabuco Canyon Road.

sycamores. The vegetation changes to palm trees and bamboo groves as the trail descends further.

Cross the bridge at Oso Parkway, turn left and head to Plaza de las Flores Center at Antonio Parkway finding your pick-up.

Modification 1: Hiking: Enter the trail at Arroyo Vista and cut the distance in half.

Modification 2: Start from Plaza de las Flores Center off Antonio Parkway. Take the Arroyo Trabuco Trail and let Loop Trail take you back to your starting point.

Trip 2: O'Neill Vista Loop
Hiking
Rating: ●●●●
Distance: 3.5 miles.
Difficulty: Moderate.
Best Time: Dry but cool season.
Access: After you enter the park (fee), leave your car in the parking lot that comes up immediately. On foot continue on the road for a short distance until you reach trailhead for Live Oak Trail on your right.

Aliso Creek Bike Path
Rating: ●●● to ●●●●
Length: Thirteen miles one way.
Difficulty: Easy
Best Time: All year, but not after rainfall.
Access: If possible take two cars and park one car at Awna Road at the entrance to Aliso and Wood Canyons Wilderness Park. From Interstate 5 take Alicia Pkwy south. After you cross Aliso Creek Road, Awna Road comes up on the right.

Park on the street (free) or in the Wilderness Park parking lot (fee). Drive up to the north end of the path close to Cook's Corner at the intersection of El Toro and Ridgeline Rd to start the ride from there for a one way trip. The advantage is that it is mostly downhill. From Interstate 5, exit El Toro Road and go towards the mountains, passing the 241 toll road. Ridgeline Road comes up on the left, turn and

Aliso Creek Bike Path, a multi-use trail

park. From 241 exit at Portola Parkway, go south, turn left on El Toro Road, park on Ridgeline Road.

The Trip: Aliso Creek Bikeway actually starts at Ridgeline Road, initially paralleling El Toro Road for about three miles. This beginning and the last part of the trail are the most scenic parts because they run along undeveloped areas.

The first part is easy to follow, but when you leave El Toro Road it can become a bit tricky due to poor sign positions. Mostly, you follow the creek paralleling it on one side or the other, crossing it over bridges.

It veers away for the first time after the bikeway passes under the Metro Link Railroad track to avoid a golf course, but rejoins it again afterwards.

It's easy to miss the access to the passage under Los Alisos Boulevard. If you get to Bough Road you have gone too far. Return and find the entrance which runs along the bottom of the channel! Be careful when you cross over the metal plate, it is slippery. After rainfalls this section is impassable. This is not the most scenic part of the ride, but it's an adventure.

After you pass under Interstate 5, which is possible only if it is dry as well, don't follow the signs to the left, instead turn right. After about 200 yards turn left to follow the (correct) signs and bike path again.

Jogging in Riley Park

After about half a mile you reach Paseo de Valencia and turn left to follow the bicycle path along the street.

You have to circumvent the city of Laguna Woods which does not allow continuation of the bike path through its boundaries. Turn right on Laguna Hills Drive. At the bottom of Laguna Hills Drive turn left into Sheep Hills Park and rejoin the Creek.

At the end of the park you turn right and then left as you enter one north end of Aliso and Woods Canyons Wilderness Park for your second scenic section. This last section is a little over three miles long and ends at Awna Road where you parked your car.

For the Hungry and Thirsty: Cook's Corner at the north end (see page 131) or eateries at the Aliso Village Center at the south end (see page 117).

Riley Wilderness Park

Rating: ●●●●
Best time: Cool season; early morning hours.
Location: 30952 Oso Parkway, Coto De Caza.
Access: From Interstate 5 exit Oso Parkway, go east for 6.5 miles, turn right into Riley Wilderness Park (fee).
Profile: The 523 acres of Riley Wilderness Park or Wagon Wheel Park were once part of the 47,432 acres of Wagon Wheel Ranch in the 1850s. Thomas F. Riley, former supervisor of the fifth district of Orange County, is to be credited for getting the land dedicated as a wilderness park. It opened in 1994.

The park offers five miles of trails for hiking, mountain biking and equestrian use. Beginning mountain bikers or families, will enjoy the park because it is an environment to learn the necessary skills. For the serious hiker and biker the park provides a good workout.

Two seasonally flowing creeks are bordered by ancient oaks and sycamores. Wildlife like mules deer, coyotes, and bobcats can be seen.

Two lookout points provide views over the rolling hills and canyons of the park and beyond to the Santa Ana Mountains. At Skink Vista point a map and guided viewer explain and point to the mountains.

Facilities: Portable restrooms close to the entrance. For equestrian use four pipe corrals,

Oak Canyon Trail in Riley Park in fall

drinking fountains, picnic tables under oaks next to the parking lot.

Special Features: One acre butterfly garden next to the visitor center. Best time to view butterflies is early June.

In addition, the park offers ranger-led tours.

For the Hungry and Thirsty: A picnic is a must under the ancient groves adjacent to the parking lot. There are also many 'wild' spots along the creeks under the trees for family picnicking. Bring your own provisions.

■ Trail Activities

Hiking, Jogging, Mountain Biking, Equestrian

Riley Loop
Mountain Biking
Rating: ●●●●

Distance: 3.3 miles or more with extensions to vista points.

Difficulty: Easy to moderate.

Best Time: Cool days during spring.

Access: Main parking lot in park.

The Ride: From the parking lot head north on Wagon Wheel Canyon Trail. This first section is shaded by riparian woodland.

At your first intersection turn left on Pheasant Run Trail which is a single track. After you turn off you cross a mostly dry creek bed and then start going up. Continue until you reach Mule Deer Trail, another single track, and turn right. Mule Deer takes you further up the mountain switching back and forth.

At the top you can turn right to Skink Vista Point with magnificent views, or go straight on a dirt road, Oak Canyon Trail. If you headed up to the Vista Point, head back and turn right on Oak Canyon Trail.

Then, take a right on Horned Toad Trail, a single track, and reach your second Vista Point with great views.

Continue on Horned Toad until it joins again with Oak Canyon Trail. Follow Oak Canyon Trail until you get back to the parking lot.

Santa Ana Mountain Trails

→ Modjeska Canyon
→ Black Star Canyon
→ Bedford Peak
→ Buena Vista Trail
→ Holy Jim Trail

■ Trail Activities

Hiking, Mountain Biking, Equestrian

Modjeska Canyon

Profile: The canyon is named after a famous Polish actress, Helena Modjeska, who moved there in 1876. Her house, Arden, from Shakespeare's 'As You Like It' is a historical landmark.

Today, the canyon is home to an eclectic mix of people who enjoy the surrounding nature.

Many trails start at Modjeska Canyon and offer opportunities for hiking, mountain biking, and horseback riding in the canyon and beyond.

Modjeska Canyon, Harding Road

Modjeska Canyon, hiking on Harding Road coming from Laurel Springs

Trip 1: Harding Road to Santiago Canyon Viewpoint
Hiking, Mountain Biking, Equestrian
Rating: ●●●●

Best Time: Cool season or early morning hours, because of permanent sun exposure.

Distance: 3.2 miles to Goat Shed and back.

Difficulty: Moderate. It is a steady uphill.

Access: From Interstate 5 take El Toro Road exit heading inland. Proceed for approximately six miles, then veer to the left onto Santiago Canyon Road.

Turn right on Modjeska Grade Road and right on Modjeska Canyon Road. Drive through the canyon following the road until you reach Tucker Wildlife Sanctuary on your right, where you park.

Facilities: Picnic tables at Goat Shed.

For the Hungry and Thirsty: Enjoy a picnic.

The Trip: Find the trailhead right across from the Tucker Wildlife Sanctuary. Pass through the gate and follow the dirt road. You can take a little detour by walking through a local plant garden. This short trail turns off to the right and takes you back to the main trail shortly after.

To your left you will see a large rock formation called Flores Peak. The story has it that in 1857 San Quentin escapee, Juan Flores, was cornered on this peak. He took a chance and jumped off the hill on his horse to escape his followers for a few more days. It must have been quite a leap considering the height of this rock.

Leave Flores peak to your left. You'll encounter a fork in the trail. Follow the dirt road uphill to the right. Enjoy several viewpoints over Harding Canyon and Santiago Canyon. As you get higher sweeping views over mountains and over the ocean can be enjoyed.

After about 45 minutes of hiking uphill, you will reach 'Goat Shed,' a picnic table under some wooden beams offering one of the best views all the way to the Temecula mountain ranges. Sit down and refresh yourself before you head back.

Modification: You can continue to Laurel Springs, which makes it an XXL hike, since you will cover 9.5 miles in all. Continue on Harding Road until a trail to your right takes you to Laurel Springs.

Other Attractions: Tucker Wildlife Sanctuary and Interpretive Center, a 12-acre non-profit nature preserve at 29322 Modjeska Canyon Road, Modjeska Canyon. In addition to serving as a research center for Cal State Fullerton University, Tucker Wildlife Sanctuary is open to the public to inform about the local wildlife and natural habitat in the Southern California canyon area. It includes a small museum, hiking trails, a small amphitheatre and picnic areas.

For the Hungry and Thirsty: Silverado Cafe is not really close but worth the drive. From Modjeska Canyon Road turn right on to Santiago Canyon Road and right again on Silverado Canyon Road. After three miles you will find Silverado Cafe on your right. The address is: 28272 Silverado Canyon Road, Silverado. Very reasonable prices!

Trip 2: Enchanted Creek - Harding Road - Harding Creek
Hiking only
Rating: ●●●●●
Best Time: When the creek is dry.
Distance: Four miles roundtrip.
Difficulty: Technical difficulty at times high; physical exertion factor low..
The Trip: You start out as in Trip 1. When you pass Flores peak on your left, take the left trail of the fork which leads to Harding Canyon. Descend to the creek bed. At the bottom of the wide valley turn right on one of the trails and follow the creek bed into the canyon.
After about one half mile the canyon narrows

A lizzard sunning on a rock

and you start going back and forth from one side of the creek to the other as you look for the easiest trails. This means that you are in the creek bed a lot hopping over increasingly big rocks and boulders.

This hike is not recommended for people with sensitive knees because you have to do a lot of climbing, bending and adjusting. Your reward is solitude in seemingly untouched enchanting nature.

After about two miles we found a perfect picnic spot at a creek bend under an ancient oak tree framed by steep canyon walls. We spent altogether three hours in the canyon and did not encounter another human soul. Instead, we saw plenty of wildlife in beautiful riparian woodland, oak groves and sycamore trees.

The trip took over two hours hiking time, but we didn't cover a lot of terrain because progress was real slow through the creek bed.

Black Star Canyon
Mountain Biking, Hiking
Rating: ●●●●●
Distance: Six miles roundtrip or longer.
Difficulty: Through the canyon easy. Uphill moderate to difficult.
Best Time: In the canyon, anytime. Up the hillside, cool season and/or early morning.
Access: From Interstate 5 take the 133 Toll Road east then the 241 Toll Road east and exit at Santiago Canyon Road. Turn right and follow

Hiking to waterfall

Santiago Canyon. Turn left on Silverado Canyon Road. Turn left on Black Star Canyon Road. After one mile you reach the vehicle gate, park to the right.

Profile: Originally, Black Star Canyon was inhabited by several different Native American tribes of which a Village Site can still be visited. Coal mining was popular for a few years under the Black Star Mining Company starting in 1879. Remains can be found.

The first part of the road passing through the canyon is private with the public having passing rights via a county easement. People living in the canyon do not like trespassers. However, the Irvine Ranch Open Space gift includes 1,988 acres that will become Black Star Canyon Wilderness Park.

The Ride: After the gate start your ride. After half a mile the road bends east and you enter Black Star Canyon. You pass by a few remote homes and through groves of ancient oaks, sycamores and eucalyptus trees. This section of the ride gently ascends through mostly shaded terrain and is therefore suited for hotter days. At the last home, after 2.5 miles, the road makes a

horseshoe bend and starts ascending seriously. You only want to do this during the cooler season. You can go up (almost) as far as you want. Each turn of the road rewards you with an even better view overlooking the Canyon, the Santa Ana Mountains and the Pacific Ocean in the distance. We made it to a private road section past a cattle gate but still had not reached the summit. We took one last good look and turned around tremendously enjoying the long downhill. Be careful not to go too fast as you might slip in the hairpin curves. Take the same way back down and out of the canyon to your car.

Combo-Trip: Bike through Black Star Canyon and Hike to the Waterfall
Biking and Hiking
Rating: ●●●●
Best Time: Any time when it is dry.
Distance: Five miles biking, 0.8 miles hiking.
Difficulty: Biking, easy, hiking moderate to difficult.
The Trip: At the bend where the serious uphill starts you can add a 0.8 mile hike to the waterfalls. Lock up your bikes. Instead of turning left on the road to the uphill, walk down

Biking in Black Star Canyon

to the creek bed and turn left climbing over boulders, scramble along the canyon walls and work your way through dense vegetation. After about 45 minutes you will reach the 50 feet high waterfalls which are mostly active after longer periods of rain. Take a break, enjoy the waterfall and pools, then turn around.

Bedford Peak
Hiking
Rating: ●●●●, for the view ●●●●●
Distance: Seven miles roundtrip.
Difficulty: Moderate to strenuous, because of elevation gain: 2000 feet in 3.5 miles. Altitude of peak: 3800 feet.
Best Time: Cool season, early morning hours. Trail is exposed to sun at all times. In winter you can end up in snow.
Access: From Interstate 5, take the 133 Toll Road north. Continue on the 241 Toll Road north and exit at Santiago Canyon. Turn right on Santiago Canyon. Go 5.5 miles to the Silverado turnoff. Turn left on Silverado, follow the road until it ends at a round-about parking area.
A Forest Adventure Pass is required and can be purchased in the Visitor Center. Bring change.

On the way to Bedford Peak

The Hike: Pass through the vehicle gate and continue up the road for about 200 yards. After you pass the big trees, there is an unmarked trail sharply going off to the left. This is the trailhead. Zig zag your way up the mountain until you pass some power lines reaching a plateau. Here the first part ends in a T-intersection. Head to the right for another two miles.
Towards the end you will reach Main Divide Road. Turn to your right and ascend a few hundred yards to Bedford Peak. Enjoy the magnificent panorama; head back the same way. A word of caution: Make sure you bring sufficient sun protection and water for this hike. Be ready for a steady and constant uphill and downhill on your return. The trail is eroded in places and there is plenty of loose rock and gravel. Bring your hiking poles! Spectacular view.

Buena Vista Trail (Santiago Trail)
Mountain Biking, Hiking
Rating: ●●●●, for the view ●●●●●
Best Time: Cool season, early morning hours, since exposed to sun.
Distance: 6.6 miles or longer.
Difficulty: Moderate, at sections strenuous (a few steep inclines).
Access: From the 405 or 5 Freeway take the 133 Toll Road going toward the mountains. Take the 241 Toll Road going south. Exit Portola Parkway and turn left. Turn right immediately at Glenn Ranch Road. Turn left on El Toro Road which becomes Santiago Canyon Road once you pass Cook's Corner on your right.
Turn right on Modjeska Grade Road and wind your way up the grade for about a mile until you reach a gate on your right which is the trailhead for Santiago Canyon Trail. Finding legal parking is not easy. We saw cars parked on the opposite side of the street about 0.2 miles down the road.
The Trip: Right after the gate, mount your

Buena Vista Traill

bikes and gradually work your way up on the trail. After about 0.2 miles, when the trail turns right running parallel with the mountain range you will be rewarded with the best continuous view possible. Especially on clear winter days, most of Orange County, some of Los Angeles County, the Pacific Ocean with Catalina and even the island of San Clemente can be seen. If you turn to the other side, the Santa Ana Mountains beckon over your shoulder.

While riding, pay attention to the trail at all times. It is washed out in many places, has deep water runoff tracks, loose gravel and some rocks. This trip is not for people suffering from vertigo as there are drop offs of several hundred feet.

Towards the end of your ride, you see Vulture Crags to your right, a rock formation where the Californian condor used to breed and where fossils can be found. A little further you come to Lookout Point. Take a break, and enjoy the spectacular view; turn around and head back.

Combo: Bike to Vulture Crag turn-off, leave your bikes and hike down to the rock and expl

If you continue for another six miles on Buena Vista Trail, you will reach Old Camp where remnants of mining activity can be found.

Holy Jim Trail
Hiking
Rating: ●●●●●
Best Time: Any time. The trail is mostly protected from the sun; very scenic, when water is coming down the falls.
Distance: 2.8 miles roundtrip - about one and a half hours.
Difficulty: Easy to moderate.
Access: Take Interstate 5 to the El Toro exit. Proceed east towards the mountains for approximately seven miles on El Toro Road. Take a right on Live Oak Canyon Road. There is no stop sign at this intersection, so look for the Cook's Corner sign to make your right turn. Take Live Oak Canyon Road a little over four miles, then pass the O'Neill Park entrance and Trabuco Canyon General Store.

The road will pass over Trabuco Creek. Pull your bike over to the large dirt clearing on the left and proceed for about 4.5 miles on the dirt road, Trabuco Creek Road (unsigned). Be sure to bring an appropriate car that can handle rocks and potholes. After the four and a half miles you'll come to a large clearing with a bulletin board. Park your car here.

Day pass for Cleveland National Forest is required, which can be purchased at Trabuco Canyon General Store.

Profile: Holy Jim Trail, which starts in Holy Jim Canyon used to be populated by beekeepers, and is named for one, James T. Smith, who was known as "old cussin' Jim" because of his colorful language. The cartographers turned the name into Holy Jim. The waterfall is a popular destination for families. Main Divide Road and Santiago Peak are destinations for serious hikers and should only be done with plenty of time and good preparation.

Special Features: Pristine waterfall. Ruins of Holy Jim's cabin.

Other Attractions: On your drive up on Trabuco Creek Road, about four miles into the area, you will see the remnants of an old mine to the left on the canyon slopes.

For the Hungry and Thirsty: Have a picnic.

The Trip: Go up the small hill to where you pass through cabins along a canyon. After the cabins you reach an iron gate where the actual trail starts. It crosses through Holy Jim Creek many times, rising gently until you reach a fork where you head right for about 1/4-mile until you reach the waterfall. The fall and pool in a grotto type surrounding provide a sense of serenity. Avoid taking this trail on vacation weekends because it becomes a "zoo" instead.

Modification1: Main Divide via Holy Jim Trail
Rating: ●●●●●
Best Time: Cool season (sun exposure).
Distance: Nine miles
Difficulty: Easy to strenuous.
The Trip: For the five mile trek to Main Divide, take the left trail at the fork. In switchbacks it will lead you up the Holy Jim Canyon. The first four miles traverse mostly sunny slopes. The last mile runs behind a ridge through a shady area with trees until you reach Main Divide opposite Bear Spring. Turn back and take the same way back.

Modification 2: Santiago Peak via Holy Jim Trail
Rating: ●●●●●
Best Time: Cool season, but bring warm clothing for climate further up.
Distance: Fifteen miles.
Difficulty: Strenuous
The Trip: At Main Divide opposite Bear Spring take Main Divide Road steadily climbing for 3 miles. It leads up to Santiago Peak at an elevation of 5687 feet. Santiago Peak is Orange County's highest Peak which offers the best view of Orange County.

Crossing a creek on Holy Jim Trail

Mission San Juan Capistrano

General Area San Juan Capistrano

→ **San Juan Creek Trail**
→ **Caspers Park**

www.sanjuancapistrano.org
www.oc-parks.com

Orientation:

The Mission San Juan Capistrano was founded in 1776 and is considered California's "Jewel of the Missions".

The City of San Juan Capistrano that developed around it is Orange County's oldest city.

The Spanish missionaries chose the valley for their seventh California mission, probably because the area offered a native population of perspective converts (the Native Americans) and sufficient fresh water and fertile land.

Today the area is not only interesting because of its beautiful mission, which has also become a cultural center, but it is also a treasure for the active person.

San Juan Capistrano is called the "equestrian capital" of the West Coast.

The city provides abundant trails for hikers, bikers and equestrians within the urban development and in the surrounding hills.

San Juan Creek Trail stretches from the northern city limits of San Juan Capistrano beyond the southern city limits all the way to the Pacific Ocean at Doheny State Beach in Dana Point (see p. 133).

Near the city borders, off Ortega highway in the Santa Ana Mountains, one of the most magnificent wilderness parks can be found.

Caspers Wilderness Park is Orange County's largest park. It offers great opportunities to those loving to exercise while enjoying the beauty of wilderness areas.

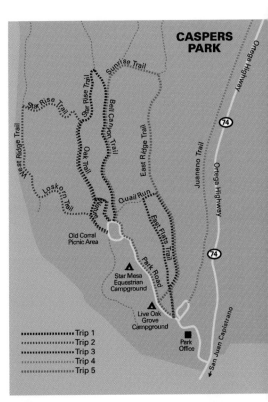

The windmill land mark at Caspers Park

Biking San Juan Creek Trail, San Juan Capistrano

■ Trail Activities
Street Biking, Mountain Biking, Hiking, Horseback Riding, Running

San Juan Creek Trail

Biking
Rating: ●●●◐
Best Time: Spring
Distance: Five miles one way.
Difficulty: Easy, good for families.
Location: Northern Trailhead at Avenida Siega and Calle Arroyo, southern trailhead at Doheny State Beach, San Juan Creek Outlet.
Access: Northern trailhead: From Interstate 5 take Ortega Highway inland to Avenida Siega; park on the street close to the corner of Calle Arroyo (free).
Southern trailhead: Exit Interstate 5 at Ortega Highway to the southwest, turn into Avenida del Obispo. Drive all the way to Dana Point Harbor.

When you cross PCH, the street is called Harbor Drive. Turn left and get to Doheny State Beach gate (fee), or turn right and drive up Park Lantern Street and park on the street at Lantern Park (free).
Profile: For bikers, this is an easy pleasant ride

Northern Trailhead of San Juan Creek Trail

Doheny State Beach, looking south

on paved bike trails, mostly along community parks and residential areas, passing by riding stables. When you do a roundtrip as a biker or do a one way from the northern trailhead as a hiker or runner, you are rewarded at the end with great views of the coastline and the ocean

Water birds near San Juan Creek mouth

at Doheny State Beach. You have the opportunity to take a swim in rather warm water; the surf is very tame here and the ocean floor does not drop off fast.

Other Attractions: A visit of Mission San Juan Capistrano is a must, if you are in the area. Parts of the original mission have been preserved, others were beautifully restored.

The mission can be visited year round. Take Ortega Highway exit, if you come on Interstate 5. You find the mission one and a half blocks from the exit on 26801 Ortega Highway.

The city is also site of the oldest neighborhood in California, Los Rios District adjacent to the train tracks, with original adobe structures that housed workers of the mission.

Facilities: San Juan Creek Trail: Water fountains, restrooms, showers, picnic tables at Doheny State Beach (see p. 133), water fountain, restrooms, picnic benches and

Star Mesa Equestrian Campground

barbecues at Descanso Park, benches and barbecues at Cook Park southwestern segment, water fountain, restrooms, benches at the northeastern segment of Cook Park near athletic fields close to the northern trailhead.

For the Hungry and Thirsty: There are concession stands with tables at Doheny State Beach. Jon's Fish Market at Dana Point Harbor is a nice choice for a lunch break (see p. 131). Or bring supplies for a picnic.

The Ride: From Doheny State Beach follow the path to San Juan Creek Outlet. You stay to the southwest side of the creek and bike inland under PCH. You will pass Obispo Park (see p. 134) and then bike for about two miles along San Juan Creek passing by Mission Bell Park. You cross a bridge for bikers, hikers and runners over Trabuco Creek.

At the juncture of Trabuco creek and San Juan Creek you take the right trail along San Juan Creek; pass under Camino Capistrano and Interstate 5, continuing along the riverbed.

Your path will leave the creek and you have to bike a short distance on Paseo Triador until you meet Calle Arroyo. There you will come to the northeastern segment of Cook Park.

You bike parallel to Calle Arroyo through the park under large trees. Cross La Novia Avenue. Horse trails parallel the bike trail close to the creek. After you pass a large area of horse stables your turn around point comes up at Avenida Siega.

Modification: Hiking, Running
For hikers or runners, who want just want to do one way, we recommend coming with two cars, if you are with a group.
Drop off one car at the beach trailhead and start at the northeastern trail head. Dropping off bikes at the northeastern trailhead and hiking up one way and biking back is another alternative.

Caspers Wilderness Park

Rating: ●●●●●
Best time: Year round.
Location: 33401 Ortega Highway, San Juan Capistrano.
Access: From the 5 Freeway in San Juan Capistrano take the 74, Ortega Highway going inland. After eight miles the entrance of Casper's Park appears on the left.
Profile: Ronald W. Caspers Regional Park encompasses 8,000 acres which makes it the largest park in the county. The park is remarkable for its size and also for its diversity of flora, fauna and geological features. Fertile valleys with live oak groves, sycamore trees seasonally running streams, wildflowers, and sage and chaparral covered hillsides characterize the park. Observe the wildlife and enjoy the vistas all the way down to the ocean. The park is ideal for hiking, biking or horseback riding with a trail system of 35 miles. 70% of the trails are open for biking.
Caspers Park is definitely one of our favorites!
Facilities: Restrooms, showers, sanitary station. An equestrian day use area, horse hitching posts and pipe corrals.
Several picnic areas, among them Old Corral Picnic Area with a windmill landmark.
Four campgrounds for tent, R.V. group and equestrian camping equipped with water, fire rings, charcoal-burning stoves.
Special Features: A Nature Center located on an observation tower presents exhibitions on the nature and history of the area, which was inhabited by Native Americans for centuries.

A thunderstorm approaches Caspers Park

Guided tours about geothermal activity and geologic features of San Juan Hot Springs are offered, as well as other guided activities such as nature walks, educational slide shows and evening programs.

For the Hungry and Thirsty: Bring your own provisions and enjoy outdoor dining under ancient oaks at one of the many picnic tables.

A Great Blue Heron in Caspers Park

■ Trail Activities
Hiking, Running, Mountain Biking, Equestrian

Trip 1: Nature Trail – Oak Trail Loop
Hiking, Running, Mountain Biking
Distance: Two miles.
Difficulty: Easy
Best Time: Anytime.
Access: After you enter the park, drive all the way to the end of the road (gate) and park close to Old Corral Picnic Area.
The Trip: This trail within Caspers Park is one of our favorites and can be easily done with the whole family. There are hardly any inclines but lots of giant oaks, and a plethora of wildlife and flora to enjoy.

Facing the gates start by turning to your left/west and find the entrance to the Nature Trail Loop along which cacti and other desert plants grow. Follow it until you see the turn off to Oak Trail while you cross a normally dry river bed. As the name indicates, old oak groves line the trail and provide shade during hot summer days.

When Oak Trail ends turn around and walk back the same way. When you reach Nature Trail Loop again go in the other direction, and enjoy the other part of the loop.

Modification: Nature Trail, Oak Trail, Bell Canyon Trail Loop

Distance: Three miles.

Difficulty: Easy

Best Time: Cool season, early morning. Bell Canyon is exposed to the sun.

Choosing this route makes the trip a bit longer. Start out with Nature Trail and Oak Trail. When Oak Trail ends, don't turn around but turn right onto Star Rise Trail.

Follow it until you reach Bell Canyon Trail. Turn right again and follow it until you reach the gates. This section is not protected from the sun by the groves, but offers nice views into the park.

Hiking Nature Trail in fall, Caspers Park

Trip 2: Loskorn Trail Loop

Hiking, Equestrian

Rating: ●●●●●

Distance: 3.5 miles.

Difficulty: Easy to moderate on the uphill.

Access: Park your car close to Old Corral Picnic Area at the end of the paved road on which you entered Caspers Park.

The Trip: Start at the south end of Nature Trail Loop until you reach Dick Loskorn Trail. Turn left and work your way up on this single path. This part of the loop is moderately strenuous but definitely worth the effort because it is so pretty. It truly gives you the sense of being away from civilization and out in the wilderness.

When you reach West Ridge Trail you can enjoy nice views. The single track ends and gives away to a truck road.

Turn right and follow it until you reach Star Rise Trail and turn right again to descend. When you reach Oak Trail turn right again to continue to Nature Trail Loop which will bring you back to your car. Watch for deer in the oak groves.

Trip 3: East Flats Trail, East Ridge Trail Loop

Hiking, Equestrian

Rating: ●●●●

Distance: Three miles.

Difficulty: Moderate

Best Time: Cool season, early morning hours

Access: After entering park go to San Juan Group Area and park. Take the paved main road further into the park. About opposite to the turn off to the ranger station is the starting point to East Flats Trail.

The Trip: East Flats Trail is a narrow trail often frequented by horse back riders. It gently elevates and offers beautiful vistas over the park and the surrounding mountains. It runs into Quail Run where you turn right to connect to East Ridge Trail.

Turn right on East Ridge and enjoy one of the most stunning views all along the way. On clear days one can see all the way to the ocean. Towards the end, East Ridge crosses East Flats. Turn left to get back to your starting point. The loop is exposed to the sun most of the way.

Biking in Bell Canyon, Caspers Park

Trip 4: Juaneno Trail
Hiking
Rating: ●●●●
Distance: 6.8 miles (XXL).You may turn around sooner.
Difficulty: Easy
Best Time: Any, since the trail is shady.
Access: After entering the park keep right and go to San Juan Group Area and park your car all the way in the back.
The Trip: Juaneno Trail is the ideal trail for sunny days because it doesn't have strenuous elevations and provides shade for most of it. Find the sign 'Juaneno Trail' and enter the trail

Deer are frequently sighted in Caspers Park

which veers off to the left of East Ridge. It meanders pleasantly through beautiful nature running parallel to Ortega Highway. The trail is 3.4 miles long. We went in for one hour and back another which provided a nice workout for us. If you do all of the seven miles round trip it takes approximately three and a half hours.

The only drawback of Juaneno Trail is its proximity to Ortega Highway. Especially on weekends and at rush hour time the revving engines can be bothersome.

Trip 5: East Loop
Mountain Biking, Hiking, Equestrian
Rating: ●●●●
Distance: 4 miles.
Difficulty: Moderate
Best Time: Cool season, early morning hours
Access: Enter the park (fee), follow the road in and park your car at Life Oak Grove Campground.
The Trip: Continue on the paved road until you reach a gate. Enter Bell Canyon Trail passing the gates. Continue on Bell Canyon which has gentle elevations but basically runs along the valley.

Turn right on Sun Rise Trail. Sun Rise takes you up to East Ridge Trail with some steep inclines. Turn right again on East Ridge where you will be rewarded with views all the way to the ocean. East Ridge stays level until the end when a steep decline brings you back to valley level. Turn right on the paved road and left into the parking lot.

Modification 1: Add Cougar Pass
Rating: ●●●●
Distance: Five miles.
Difficulty: Moderate to strenuous.
The Trip: This Loop can be extended by taking Cougar Pass which turns off Sun Rise Trail at the very beginning. Follow Cougar pass and turn right on East Ridge Trail which takes you to the highest point, about 900 feet, with the best views of the park. This route is about one mile longer and gives you a cardio workout.

Photographs

M. Biemann: Cover, 5, 198

V. E. Bondybey: 10, 19, 21, 26, 27, 34, 38, 40, 44, 71, 78, 79, 86, 87, 90, 99, 111, 116, 119, 129, 134, 136, 147, 195

N. Fischer: Cover, 8, 12, 16, 17, 18, 19, 20, 21, 23, 24, 25, 26, 27, 28, 30, 31,32, 33, 34, 35, 36, 37, 38, 39, 41, 42, 43, 50, 51, 52, 53, 54, 55, 56, 57, 58, 59, 60, 61, 62, 63, 64, 65, 66, 67, 68, 69, 70, 71, 72, 73, 74, 75, 76, 77, 78, 79, 80, 81, 82, 83, 84, 86, 87, 88, 89, 91, 92, 93, 95, 96, 97, 98, 99, 100, 101, 102, 103, 104, 105, 106, 107, 108, 109, 110, 112, 113, 117, 120, 122, 123, 124, 125, 126, 127, 128, 130, 131, 132, 133, 134, 135, 137, 138, 139, 140, 141,142, 143, 144, 145, 146, 147, 155, 160, 161, 165, 168, 170, 173, 176, 179, 185, 186, 188, 200, 201, 202, 203, 205

V. Ferez: 155, 156, 157, 169, 177, 181, 183, 187, 191

S. Gahlert: 166

G. Gamboa: 48

H. J. Gamboa: 45, 46, 48, 49, 76, 85, 93, 113, 116, 117, 118, 150, 151, 152, 153, 156, 158, 159, 160, 162, 163, 164, 166, 167, 169, 170, 171, 172, 174, 175, 176, 178, 180, 182, 188, 189, 190, 192, 193, 194, 196, 197, 204, 206, 207

J. D. Gamboa: 10, 48, 159, 192

K. Neunstoecklin: 10

G. Smith: 22, 148, 149, 199

Sport im Bild, 1924: 14

Active in Orange County

Published by f+b Verlag, Eching, Germany
Copyright© 2010 by f+b Verlag
Maps Copyright© 2010 by f+b Verlag
First Published: September 2010

ISBN 978-3-806671-2-8

Design: Klaus Neunstoecklin
Map Design: Francie Buschur
Title Design: Klaus Neunstoecklin, Photo: Nanda Fischer
Photo Editor: Agentur Bresser, Klaus Neunstoecklin

Printed in The United States by Delta Printing Solutions